PENITENTIAL SERVICES

Oliver Crilly
Editor

the columba press

TWENTY-THIRD PUBLICATIONS
XXIII P.O. Box 180 • Mystic, CT 06355 • 1-800-321-0411

Second Printing 1997

Twenty-Third Publications
185 Willow Street
P.O. Box 180
Mystic, CT 06355
(860) 536-2611
800-321-0411

ISBN 0-89622-554-2
Library of Congress Catalog Card Number 92-83741
Printed in the U.S.A.

Columba Press ISBN 1 85607 061 1

CONTENTS

INTRODUCTION

Reflecting on the forgiveness of Mehmet Ali Agca by Pope John Paul II, *Time* magazine quoted John Dryden: "Forgiveness to the injured doth belong." Deeds are done by individuals, said the *Time* writer, and must be judged individually. There is a sense in which that represents a part of the church's understanding of her own discipline of reconciliation. The individual must seek forgiveness; the acts of the penitent are an essential part of the celebration of the sacrament of reconciliation:

> Reconciliation of individual penitents is the only normal and ordinary way of celebrating the sacrament. (*Reconciliatio et Paenitentia*, paragraph 32)

The church's tradition of reconciliation goes far beyond the one-to-one confrontation indicated by the magazine writer, of course. In the understanding of the church, reconciliation has been achieved by the sacrifice of Christ, and all reconciliation in the church's daily practice is rooted in Christ's reconciliation:

> It is all God's work. It was God who reconciled us to himself through Christ and gave us the work of handing on this reconciliation. (2 Corinthians 5:18)

In the *Rite of Penance*, the church envisages, as well as the ordinary one-to-one celebration of the sacrament, a communal celebration concluding with individual confession and absolution (Rite 2), and, in very exceptional and carefully regulated circumstances, general confession and absolution (Rite 3). Rite 2 is considered as just as normal a celebration as Rite 1:

> The second form—reconciliation of a number of penitents with individual confession and absolution—even though in the preparatory acts it helps to give greater emphasis to the community aspects of the sacrament, is the same as the first form in the culminating sacramental

act, namely, individual confession and individual absolution of sins. It can thus be regarded as equal to the first form as regards the normality of the rite. (*Reconciliatio et Paenitentia*, paragraph 32)

What the Apostolic Exhortation calls "the community aspects of the sacrament" have received greater expression in pastoral practice in recent years, and the need for resource material for communal celebrations has increased. That is one reason for the present publication, which makes no claim either to be exhaustive or to impose its outline celebrations rigidly. It is more like a quarry from which people may draw away the blocks that suit their purposes in order to build up the particular celebration that corresponds to the pastoral needs of their own place and time. If a celebrant finds that a complete outline fills his need on a given occasion, and he is saved some time and energy in researching further, that is a bonus, and we will be glad to have been of assistance.

One other aspect of these penitential celebrations may be worth reflecting on. They offer the opportunity to small groups, perhaps even families, and to larger parish groups, to reflect prayerfully on our continuing need for forgiveness and for healing and reconciliation. In this context, many of the celebrations need not necessarily end with sacramental confession and absolution. Something like the penitential rite at Mass might very well suffice on a particular occasion, leaving the participants to seek sacramental reconciliation later on their own time. Whether there is sacramental confession or not, the emphasis on the ongoing need for forgiveness is a valuable part of what takes place—a call to conversion and a reassurance of God's faithful love and faithful forgiveness.

From time to time, a priest might also consider it useful to use some of these outlines (or parts of them) as an aid to preparation for confession, just before the ordinary Saturday confessions in the parish.

Dr. Haddon Willmer has written and lectured a good deal on "the politics of forgiveness." He is referring not only to the need for forgiveness in the political arena, but to our need to locate the experience of forgiveness in the reality of our daily lives, rather than locking it away in a ritual remoteness. Forgiveness is accepting our own limitations, those of those around us, and those of the situation in which we find ourselves.

Forgiveness is difficult. Yet every time we seek forgiveness we are called to forgive each other, to see each other today without the burden of yesterday's grudges, to get up today without yesterday's anger. Forgiveness is difficult, just as genuine love is difficult, because it is unconditional. Chiara Lubich has a beautiful phrase for it: She has referred to forgiveness as "amnesty in the heart": "... forgiving seventy times seven, drawing close to all with this complete amnesty in the heart, with this universal forgiveness" (New City magazine). We need to provide more occasions where people can reflect, prayerfully and under the guidance of the word of God in the Scriptures, on the need for this ongoing forgiveness in our lives, and on the generosity with which God offers us healing and reconciliation. Gathered together in this book is the written summary of how some people have tried to structure simple occasions of reflection and of celebration when we invite God's healing and forgiving love into our lives. We hope they will prove useful.

Oliver Crilly

OUTLINE STRUCTURE OF PENITENTIAL SERVICES

Some of the services in this book are sacramental and some of them are intended just as a prayerful reflection on forgiveness and reconciliation, perhaps with some symbolic content, and sometimes concluding with a simple prayer for forgiveness, like the penitential rite from the beginning of the Mass. It is not necessary to fit them all into one category, or to envisage only one unchanging structure for them. However, for the sacramental penitential services, which correspond to Rite 2 of the *Rite of Penance*, a basic structure is given in the Introduction to the *Rite*. A summary appears below. Further details may be checked by referring to the text of the *Rite* itself. The *Rite* also contains a variety of suitable texts that would enrich any service.

Summary of Structure

Introductory Rites
  Entrance Hymn
  Sign of the Cross
  Greeting
  Introduction
  Opening Prayer

Celebration of the Word of God
  Scripture Readings
  Homily
  Examination of Conscience

Liturgy of Reconciliation
  Form of General Confession (e.g. Confiteor)
  Litany or Song (of contrition, forgiveness, God's mercy)
  The Our Father (which is never omitted)
  Individual Confession and Absolution
  Exhortation (to thanksgiving and good works)
  Praise for God's Mercy (psalm, hymn, litany, e.g. Magnificat)
  Concluding Prayer of Thanksgiving

Concluding Rite
  Blessing
  Dismissal

ADVENT I

Oliver Crilly

Theme: Toward the coming of the Lord

Opening Hymn and Enthronement of the Book
As the opening hymn is sung, the presider, readers, homilist, confessors, and servers enter in procession with the lectionary, solemnly enthrone it on the lectern, and the presider incenses it.

P In the name of the Father, and of the Son, and of the Holy Spirit.

R Amen.

P The grace of our Lord Jesus Christ
and the love of God
and the fellowship of the Holy Spirit
be with you all.

R And also with you.

P Let us pray to God our Father
that we may sincerely call to mind our sins
as we wait in joyful hope
for the coming of our Savior Jesus Christ.

Pause for silent prayer.

P All praise to you, almighty Father,
fountain of all holiness.
You so loved the world
that you sent your only Son
that we might know your will
for our salvation.
Help us to live in faith and love
as we wait in hope till he comes again.
We ask this through Jesus Christ our Lord.

R Amen.

THE LITURGY OF THE WORD

First Reading   Titus 2:11–14

A reading from the letter of Paul to Titus.

God's grace has been revealed, and it has made salvation possible for the whole human race and taught us that what we have to do is to give up everything that does not lead to God, and all our worldly ambitions; we must be self-restrained and live good and religious lives here in this present world, while we are waiting in hope for the blessing which will come with the Appearing of the glory of our great God and Savior Christ Jesus. He sacrificed himself for us in order to *set us free from all wickedness* and *to purify a people so that it could be his very own* and would have no ambition except to do good.

The word of the Lord.

R   Thanks be to God.

Second Reading   1 Peter 1:3, 4, 6, 7

A reading from the first letter of Peter.

Blessed be God the Father of our Lord Jesus Christ, who in his great mercy has given us a new birth as his sons, by raising Jesus Christ from the dead, so that we have a sure hope and the promise of an inheritance that can never be spoiled or soiled and never fade away, because it is being kept for you in the heavens.

This is a cause of great joy for you, even though you may for a short time have to bear being plagued by all sorts of trials; so that, when Jesus Christ is revealed, your faith will have been tested and proved like gold—only it is more precious than gold, which is corruptible even though it bears testing by fire—and then you will have praise and glory and honor.

The word of the Lord.

R   Thanks be to God.

A short period of silence follows, for personal reflection.

Gospel Matthew 25:31–40

A reading from the holy Gospel according to Matthew.

"When the Son of Man comes in his glory, escorted by all the angels, then he will take his seat on his throne of glory. All the nations will be assembled before him and he will separate men one from another as the shepherd separates sheep from goats. He will place the sheep on his right hand and the goats on his left. Then the King will say to those on his right hand, 'Come, you whom my Father has blessed, take for your heritage the kingdom prepared for you since the foundation of the world. For I was hungry and you gave me food; I was thirsty and you gave me drink; I was a stranger and you made me welcome; naked and you clothed me, sick and you visited me, in prison and you came to see me.' Then the virtuous will say to him in reply, 'Lord, when did we see you hungry and feed you; or thirsty and give you drink? When did we see you a stranger and make you welcome; naked and clothe you; sick or in prison and go to see you?' And the King will answer, 'I tell you solemnly, in so far as you did this to one of the least of these brothers of mine, you did it to me.'"

The gospel of the Lord.

R   Praise to you, Lord Jesus Christ.

Homily

The homily leads to an examination of conscience and is followed by a period of silence for personal reflection.

THE SACRAMENT OF PENANCE

P   My brothers and sisters, confess your sins and pray for each other that you may be healed.

All   I confess to almighty God...*(all pray the confiteor)*

P   Let us now pray to the Father in the words our Savior gave us:

All   Our Father...

Sign of Peace

P As brothers and sisters in Christ,
reconciled with one another before God,
let us offer each other a sign of peace.

Individual Confession

Reflective music may be played during individual confession, with adequate periods of prayerful silence. There should be enough priests available to conclude the confessions in a reasonable time, but if numbers for confession are very large, the final prayer and blessing may be said after a fixed period, with confessors continuing afterward for the rest of the congregation.

Praise of God's Mercy   Ephesians 1:11–14

And it is in him that we were claimed as God's own,
chosen from the beginning,
under the predetermined plan of the one who guides all things
as he decides by his own will;
chosen to be,
for his greater glory,
the people who would put their hopes in Christ before he came.
Now you too, in him,
have heard the message of the truth and the good news of your
    salvation,
and have believed it;
and you too have been stamped with the seal of the Holy Spirit of
    the Promise,
the pledge of our inheritance
which brings freedom for those whom God has taken for his own,
to make his glory praised.

Final Prayer

P All thanks and praise to you, almighty Father, God of compassion and mercy. May we who have again received your endless

mercy and forgiveness go out from here now to show your love and compassion to all those we meet, that the world may know the glory of your Son.
We ask this through Christ our Lord.

R   Amen.

Blessing

P   May almighty God bless you, the Father, and the Son, ✠ and the Holy Spirit.

R   Amen.

Dismissal

P   Go in peace to love and serve the Lord.

R   Thanks be to God.

ADVENT II

Jack McArdle, ss cc

Note: Parts I, II, and III should be limited to five minutes each.

PART I: **Gospel Reading**   John 1:15–39

A reading from the holy Gospel according to John.

John appears as his witness. He proclaims:
"This is the one of whom I said:
He who comes after me
ranks before me
because he existed before me."

Indeed, from his fullness we have, all of us, received—
yes, grace in return for grace,
since, though the Law was given through Moses,
grace and truth have come through Jesus Christ.
No one has ever seen God;
it is the only Son, who is nearest to the Father's heart,
who has made him known.

When the Jews sent priests and Levites from Jerusalem to ask [John], "Who are you?" he not only declared, but he declared quite openly, "I am not the Christ." "Well, then," they asked, "are you Elijah?" "I am not," he said. "Are you the Prophet?" He answered, "No." So they said to him, "Who are you? We must take back an answer to those who sent us. What have you to say about yourself?" So John said, "I am, as Isaiah prophesied:

> *a voice that cries in the wilderness:*
> *Make a straight way for the Lord."*

Now these men had been sent by the Pharisees, and they put this further question to him, "Why are you baptizing if you are not the Christ, and not Elijah, and not the prophet?" John replied, "I baptize with water; but there stands among you—unknown to you—the one who is coming after me; and I am not fit to undo his sandal strap." This happened at Bethany, on the far side of the Jordan, where John was baptizing.

The next day, seeing Jesus coming toward him, John said, "Look, there is the lamb of God that takes away the sin of the world. This is the one I spoke of when I said: A man is coming after me who ranks before me because he existed before me. I did not know him myself, and yet it was to reveal him to Israel that I came baptizing with water." John also declared, "I saw the Spirit coming down on him from heaven like a dove and resting on him. I did not know him myself, but he who sent me to baptize with water had said to me, 'The man on whom you see the Spirit come down and rest is the one who is going to baptize with the Holy Spirit.' Yes, I have seen and I am the witness that he is the Chosen One of God."

On the following day as John stood there again with two of his disciples, Jesus passed, and John stared hard at him and said, "Look, there is the lamb of God." Hearing this, the two disciples followed Jesus. Jesus turned around, saw them following and said, "What do you want?" They answered, "Rabbi,"—which means Teacher— "where do you live?" "Come and see," he replied; so they went and saw where he lived, and stayed with him the rest of that day. It was about the tenth hour.

The gospel of the Lord.

R   Praise to you, Lord Jesus Christ.

Reflection

Preparing the manger of our hearts for the coming of Jesus. Listening to John the Baptist calling on us to prepare the way of the Lord, to make straight the Lord's path. Asking the Spirit of God to switch on the full beam of light in our hearts—to show up and reveal the sins, the flaws, the hurts, the resentments, the weaknesses that make my heart and soul an unfit place for God to dwell.

Pause for quiet meditation—a version of Prepare Ye the Way of the Lord.

PART II **Gospel Reading**   Luke 2:1–7

A reading from the holy Gospel according to Luke.

Now at this time Caesar Augustus issued a decree for a census of the whole world to be taken. This census—the first—took place while Quirinius was governor of Syria, and everyone went to his own town to be registered. So Joseph set out from the town of Nazareth in Galilee and traveled up to Judaea, to the town of David called Bethlehem, since he was of David's House and line, in order to be registered together with Mary, his betrothed, who was with child. While they were there the time came for her to have her child, and she gave birth to a son, her first-born. She wrapped him in swaddling clothes, and laid him in a manger because there was no room for them at the inn.

The gospel of the Lord.

R   Praise to you, Lord Jesus Christ.

Reflection

There was no room for him—many people just didn't want to know. They had no time. They couldn't be bothered. At least they had some excuse—they just didn't know. Even on the cross Jesus would ask the Father to forgive those who were killing him—because they didn't know either.

We certainly cannot claim that excuse. What a tragedy if, 2000 years later, we still have no time, can't be bothered, just don't want to know. Until such time as we throw open the doors of our hearts and souls and invite Jesus to come and live there—until that time, we cannot have any meaning or any sincerity in celebrating Christmas. What would Jesus discover in your heart if you opened the doors now and invited him in?

Pause for reflection with quiet "mood" music.

PART III **Gospel Reading**   John 1:10–13

A reading from the holy Gospel according to John.

He was in the world
that had its being through him,
and the world did not know him.
He came to his own domain
and his own people did not accept him.
But to all who did accept him
he gave power to become children of God,
to all who believe in the name of him
who was born not out of human stock
or urge of the flesh
or will of man
but of God himself.

The gospel of the Lord.

R   Praise to you, Lord Jesus Christ.

Reflection

"He came to his own domain and his own people did not accept him. But to all who did accept him he gave power to become children of God." He came as a Savior and Redeemer—and he came to forgive sinners and to free slaves to sin. He invited us into the family, children of God, able to call God Father, Abba, Daddy.

Christmas is a time for homecoming. We all like to be with our families at Christmas, if we can. Even the day after Christmas is often spent visiting our extended family—grandparents, cousins, and so on.

Jesus is inviting you home for Christmas. You may be a real Prodigal, but he assures you of the Father's hug. Come to Jesus now and tell him that you want to come home, that you want to start again. Let this be a real Christmas, when like a poor shepherd who has just been told the Good News, you run to Bethlehem to kneel at a manger, to welcome a Savior. You may have longed for such an event, for such a coming. That is nothing compared to the intense longing in the heart of Jesus for you to come to him. Now there's joy in heaven—the sinner and the Savior are meeting.

Music: "Joy to the World," or another appropriate song.

PART IV Individual Celebration of the Sacrament

Those coming forward to celebrate the sacrament could be encouraged to begin in one of the following ways.

1. "I want to come home to God's family for Christmas, because I have wandered away when I ..."

2. "I wish to invite Jesus into the stable of my heart and soul, and I ask his forgiveness and his freedom from bondage because of what he finds there ..."

3. "In this time of Advent, I want to begin all over again, because I ..."

Suggestion: *As people go forward for the sacrament, there should be a minister to help maintain an atmosphere of prayer and of prayerful quiet, with an occasional short prayer, a little reminder of what's happening, and appropriate music for a prayerful atmosphere.*

Just keep things flowing gently and with an atmosphere of warmth and love.

PART V Conclusion

It is ideal if all ministers of the sacrament gather around the altar at the beginning. Then at the end of Part III they go to their places of ministry. At the end of the service they return to the altar for a communal prayer of penance, a final blessing, and dismissal.

ADVENT III

Catherine Gorman

Theme: Responding to God's call to conversion and renewal

Gathering

As the people gather, each one is met at the church door and given the text of the hymns, the assembly's responses, and a candle. Suitable lighting (dimmed lights focusing on the ambo and the cross), artwork (banners depicting Advent and reconciliation themes, e.g. waiting, light, and darkness, the words "Marantha: Come Lord Jesus," "Come Back To Me," etc.), and the arrangement of flowers and candles at the places designated for individual confession, can help to foster a welcoming atmosphere.

Introduction

Presider:

The grace of our Lord Jesus Christ, the love of God, and the fellowship of the Holy Spirit, be with you all.

R   And also with you.

P   In these four weeks of Advent each year, we are reminded that we are called to be a people living in joyful hope, waiting for the time when Christ will come again in glory. The Scriptures we hear during these weeks remind us that we are to be ready for Christ whenever he comes, for we know not the day or the hour. We have gathered here together now, to think about our lives and our commitment to living in joyful hope, waiting for Christ. We will spend some time listening to God's word in Scripture, a word that calls us to renewal, to forgiveness, and to peace.

As we begin our liturgy, we light our wreath. *(While the wreath is being lit...)* In the middle of this, the darkest time of the year, we, as a church, light candles, reminding us that, in the darkest of nights, Christ is our light, a light no darkness can overcome. At this time of year when everything in nature is dying, we focus on an evergreen wreath, reminding us that God is ever present to us, even in the midst of death.

In this spirit of hopefulness and trust, we sing our opening hymn, the text of which reminds us that God's word lives within each of our hearts, if we but have the ears to hear it.

Hymn

Sing "Song For a Young Prophet" (based on Jeremiah 1, Damian Lundy, Songs of the Spirit*), or another appropriate hymn.*

Opening Prayer

Gracious and Merciful God, your love for us knows no bounds. Open our eyes as we come before you now, that we may see ourselves as you see us. Give us wisdom that we may recognize our need for your forgiveness, and so celebrate your gift of reconciling peace.
We make our prayer through Christ our Lord.

R   Amen.

Liturgy of the Word and Examination of Conscience

Presider:
I invite you now to sit comfortably as we listen and respond to God's word.

First Reading   Exodus 34:4–6, 8–9

A reading from the book of Exodus.

And so Moses cut two tablets of stone like the first and, with the two tablets of stone in his hands, he went up the mountain of Sinai in the early morning as Yahweh had commanded him. And Yahweh descended in the form of a cloud, and Moses stood with him there.

He called on the name of Yahweh. Yahweh passed before him and proclaimed, "Yahweh, Yahweh, a God of tenderness and compassion, slow to anger, rich in kindness and faithfulness." And Moses bowed down to the ground at once and worshiped. "If I have indeed won your favor, Lord," he said, "let my Lord come with us, I beg. True, they are a headstrong people, but forgive us our faults and our sins, and adopt us as your heritage."

The word of the Lord.

R   Thanks be to God.

Responsorial Psalm

You might like to choose one of the following:
"Have Mercy Lord," (Psalm 51), "Out of the Depths," (Psalm 130), "I Lift Up My Soul," (Psalm 25), "The Cry of the Poor," (Psalm 34), "You Are Near," (Psalm 139, St. Louis Jesuits, Glory and Praise, II)

Second Reading   1 John 1:8–9; 2:1–2

A reading from the first letter of John.

If we say that we have no sin in us,
we are deceiving ourselves
and refusing to admit the truth;
but if we acknowledge our sins,
then God who is faithful and just
will forgive our sins and purify us
from everything that is wrong.

I am writing this, my children,
to stop you sinning;
but if anyone should sin,
we have our advocate with the Father,
Jesus Christ, who is just;
he is the sacrifice that takes our sins away,
and not only ours,
but the whole world's.

The word of the Lord.

R   Thanks be to God.

Gospel Acclamation

John 8:12

Alleluia, alleluia.
Jesus said:
"I am the light of the world;
anyone who follows me will not be walking in the dark;
he will have the light of life."
Alleluia.

Gospel

John 3:16–22

A reading from the holy Gospel according to John.

God loved the world so much
that he gave his only Son,
so that everyone who believes in him may not be lost
but may have eternal life.
For God sent his Son into the world
not to condemn the world,
but so that through him the world might be saved.
No one who believes in him will be condemned;
but whoever refuses to believe is condemned already,
because he has refused to believe
in the name of God's only Son.
On these grounds is sentence pronounced:
that though the light has come into the world
men have shown they prefer
darkness to the light
because their deeds were evil.
And indeed, everybody who does wrong
hates the light and avoids it,
for fear his actions should be exposed;
but the man who lives by the truth
comes out into the light,
so that it may be plainly seen that what he does is done in God.

The gospel of the Lord.

R   Praise to you, Lord Jesus Christ.

Homily Suggestions

Introduction: *The Word of God, which lives in each of our hearts, calls us to reflect on our relationship with God, and with those who are a part of our lives. Invite those assembled to take a while to look at the various areas of their lives, and bring them into the healing light of God's forgiveness.*

An examination of conscience follows, which may be based on the Gospel images of darkness and light and applied to our relationship with God, with others, and with oneself.

If this liturgy is celebrated in small groups, the following may be included at this point:

All present have pens and paper, and are now invited to write about their anxieties and their failings, based on their examination of conscience. Allow about ten minutes for this exercise. Encourage all to write as they would to a trusted friend, or if they wish, to address the "letter" to God. Quiet, instrumental music can be helpful during this time. These letters are given to the priest during the time of individual confession, and are burned after the liturgy. The penitents may refer to the contents of their letter during their confession. Time, and the number of priests and penitents, will obviously be influencing factors.

Renewal of Baptismal Vows and Individual Confession

Having examined our attitudes and our lifestyle, we now renew our baptismal promises, the vows that bind us to God as sons and daughters, and to each other as sisters and brothers. Through baptism, we became children of the light, for God called us out of darkness into the light of Christ Jesus, the light of the world.

Tapers are lit from the Advent wreath, and the light is shared among the assembly. An appropriate hymn may be sung during this time, e.g. "The Lord Is My Light," (Taizé), "What You Hear in the Dark," (St. Louis Jesuits, Earthen Vessels), "The Light of Christ," (Donald Fishel, Songs of the Spirit).

When all candles are lit:

Presider:

Let us now profess our faith in God, our commitment to the church, and our service to one another.

P   Do you reject Satan?

R   I do.

P   And all his works?

R   I do.

P   And all his empty promises?

R   I do.

P   Do you believe in God, the Father Almighty, Creator of Heaven and Earth?

R   I do.

P   Do you believe in Jesus Christ, God's only son, our Lord who was born of the Virgin Mary, was crucified, died, and was buried, rose from the dead, and is now seated at the right hand of the Father?

R   I do.

P   In your relationships with others:
Are you willing to grow in your understanding of Christ's gospel, and to proclaim his Good News by your words and your actions?

R   I am, with God's help.

P   Are you willing to respect the dignity of all, to exercise justice, and to strive for peace in your relationships with others?

R   I am, with God's help.

P   We have confessed our faith, and now, as we prepare to confess our sinfulness, we say together:

All   Glory be to the Father, and to the Son, and to the Holy Spirit, as it was in the beginning, is now, and ever shall be, world without end.
Amen.

As the penitents go to individual confession, they place their candles (still lit) in an appropriate container of sand, which has been placed beside each confessor. There are many appropriate hymns that may be sung at this time.

Concluding Rite

When all have returned to their seats:

Presider:
Loving Creator, and Giver of everything that is good, we have repented of our sins and have received your forgiveness.

Strengthen our resolve to listen to your word, not only during this Advent season, but throughout the year that lies ahead, so that we may grow in our relationship with you.

We make our prayer through your Son, our Lord Jesus Christ, in the power of the Holy Spirit, One God forever and ever.

R   Amen.

LENT I

Brian Magee, CM

Opening Hymn

Music should be chosen to suit the congregation. Additional hymns and psalms may be chosen and used in other parts of the service.

Introduction

P   Grace, mercy, and peace be with you from God the Father and Christ Jesus our Savior.

R   And also with you.

P   During this time of renewal, we are called in a special way to remember our baptism. This time of Lent is especially given to the celebration of baptism. Throughout the Christian world, many thousands are preparing to be baptized at Easter, and each of us is called to join with them by renewing our own baptism. We have first to remember our own baptism—something that is difficult for most of us because we were baptized as infants. But I remember through knowing what the sacrament should mean for me in my daily living now. In that remembering I come to know how I should be living as a Christian and how far I am from that ideal. And renewal means repenting of my failure and resolving once more to live by the promises once made for me by my parents and godparents. Let us begin by prayer for that grace.

Prayer

P   Let us pray.
Lord our God, you have called us to be a chosen race, a royal priesthood, a consecrated nation, a people set apart. You have

called us out of darkness into your wonderful light. We acknowledge that we have not lived up to our calling, but have sinned before you.
Renew once more, through the tears of repentance, the grace that came to us in the water of baptism.
We ask this through Christ our Lord.

R   Amen.

First Reading   Joshua 24:1–2, 15–25

Through our baptism, we choose to serve the Lord, our God. Living our baptism means putting away all temptations to follow other gods.

A reading from the book of Joshua.

Joshua gathered all the tribes of Israel together at Shechem; then he called the elders, leaders, judges and scribes of Israel, and they presented themselves before God. Then Joshua said to all the people: "But if you will not serve Yahweh, choose today whom you wish to serve, whether the gods that your ancestors served beyond the River, or the gods of the Amorites in whose land you are now living. As for me and my House, we will serve Yahweh."

The people answered, "We have no intention of deserting Yahweh and serving other gods! Was it not Yahweh our God who brought us and our ancestors out of the land of Egypt, the house of slavery, who worked those great wonders before our eyes and preserved us all along the way we traveled and among all the peoples through whom we journeyed? We too will serve Yahweh, for he is our God."

The Joshua said to the people, "You cannot serve Yahweh, because he is a holy God who will not forgive your transgressions or your sins. If you desert Yahweh to follow alien gods he in turn will afflict and destroy you after the goodness he has shown you." The people answered Joshua, "No; it is Yahweh we wish to serve." Then Joshua said to the people, "You are witnesses against yourselves that you have chosen Yahweh, to serve him." They answered, "We are witnesses." "Then cast away the alien gods among you and give your hearts to Yahweh the God of Israel!" The people answered Joshua, "It is Yahweh our God we choose to serve; it is his voice that we will obey."

That day, Joshua made a covenant for the people.

The word of the Lord.

R   Thanks be to God.

Responsorial Psalm   Psalm 126

R   What marvels indeed he did for us,
      and how overjoyed we were!

1.   When Yahweh brought Zion's captives home,
      at first it seemed like a dream;
      then our mouths filled with laughter,
      and our lips with song. R

2.   Even the pagans started talking
      about the marvels Yahweh had done for us!
      What marvels indeed he did for us,
      and how overjoyed we were! R

3.   Yahweh, bring all our captives back again
      like torrents in the Negeb!
      Those who went sowing in tears
      now sing as they reap. R

4.   They went away, went away weeping,
      carrying the seed;
      they come back, come back singing,
      carrying their sheaves. R

Second Reading   Romans 6:3-4, 8-11

We are reborn into the family of God through baptism; we should be no longer dead through sin.

A reading from the letter of Paul to the Romans.

You have been taught that when we were baptized in Christ Jesus we were baptized in his death; in other words, when we were baptized we went into the tomb with him and joined him in death, so that as Christ was raised from the dead by the Father's glory, we too might live a new life.

But we believe that having died with Christ we shall return to life with him: Christ, as we know, having been raised from the dead will never die again. Death has no power over him any more. When he died, he died, once for all, to sin, so his life now is life with God; and in that way, you too must consider yourselves to be dead to sin but alive for God in Christ Jesus.

The word of the Lord.

R   Thanks be to God.

Acclamation

Glory and praise to you, O Christ!
God loved the world so much
that God gave his only Son;
everyone who believes in him has eternal life.
Glory and praise to you, O Christ!

Gospel   John 3:16–21

A reading from the holy Gospel according to John.

God loved the world so much
that he gave his only Son,
so that everyone who believes in him may not be lost
but may have eternal life.
For God sent his Son into the world
not to condemn the world,
but so that through him the world might be saved.
No one who believes in him will be condemned;
whoever refuses to believe is condemned already,
because he has refused to believe
in the name of God's only Son.

On these grounds is sentence pronounced:
that though the light has come into the world
men have shown they prefer
darkness to the light
because their deeds were evil.
And indeed, everybody who does wrong
hates the light and avoids it,
for fear his actions should be exposed;
but the man who lives by the truth
comes out into the light,
so that it may be plainly seen that what he does is done in God.

The gospel of the Lord.

R   Praise to you, Lord Jesus Christ.

Suggestions for Homily

Most communities of believers live in a world that is mainly pagan, just as the first Christians did. It is a world that does not understand the Christian way of living, and is often hostile to it. Those first Christians were often reminded that they should show their distinctiveness by a higher moral code. They were a people called to holiness through the baptism that had separated them from the unbeliever. St. Clement reminded them that "we have to keep our baptism pure and undefiled." He was, of course, speaking to Christians who had gone through a long process of preparing for baptism. They were people who saw the difference between their present way of life and what they had once been. They had renounced Satan and sin, they had made solemn promises. They recognized that they were now dead to sin and alive to Jesus Christ. To fail through sin would be a great shame and be unexpected. In time, the Christian community did have those who failed, those whom St. Cyprian described as having "broken their oath to Christ."

But the church has always recognized that receiving baptism means entering into a distinctive way of life that calls for rejecting sin and being committed to virtue.

One of the signs that Christians began a new life at baptism was in the reclothing of the person who had gone down into the baptismal pool and been washed clean of the past life. The new white clothes given then symbolized a new person coming out of that font. St. Paul refers to this when he says: "You have stripped off your old behavior with your old self and you have put on a new self." The tradition of the white garment or baptismal robe stays with us. We all had the white garment placed on us while the priest said to each of us: "You have become a new creation, and have clothed yourself in Christ. See in this white garment the outward sign of your Christian dignity. With your family and friends to help you by word and example, bring that dignity unstained into the everlasting life of heaven."

We give a real meaning to our baptism when we try to live a sinless life. But, more positively, we find that real meaning in a life of Christian standards, when we live as Christ called us to, when we live as he lived. The wish of the priest at the giving of the white garment significantly reminds us that we cannot do it alone. We belong to a community, we are baptized into a body. We are called to be members one of another, to live a life of love. We support each other by word and example; and we can fail each other in the same way.

And we do fail to live up to the gospel standards. Our identity through baptism is as a follower of Christ and his way. Each year at Lent (or at our annual retreat) we try to recommit ourselves to that standard, to confess our past failures, and to renew once more our baptismal promises. Let us now take time to look at the demands of the gospel for us, before we confess our failures.

Examination of Conscience

St. Paul wrote to his new Christians at Colossae to remind them that, being raised up with Christ, they must live a life hidden with Christ in God. He spells out for them what it means to be dead to sin. Let us examine ourselves by his standards: (Colossians 3:5-4:5)

You must kill everything in you that belongs only to earthly life: fornication, impurity, guilty passion, evil desires and especially greed, which is the same thing as worshiping a false god.

You must give all these things up: getting angry, being bad-tempered, spitefulness, abusive language and dirty talk; and never tell each other lies.

You should be clothed in sincere compassion, in kindness and humility, gentleness and patience. Bear with one another; forgive each other as soon as a quarrel begins.

Let the message of Christ, in all its richness, find a home with you.

With gratitude in your hearts sing psalms and hymns and inspired songs to God.

[Wives, love and respect your husbands. Husbands, love and respect your wives; treat one another with gentleness.]

Children, be obedient to your parents always, because that is what will please the Lord.

Parents, never drive your children to resentment or you will make them feel frustrated.

[Employers], make sure that your [workers]are given what is just and fair.

Whatever your work is, put your heart into it as if it were for the Lord.

Be persevering in your prayers and be thankful as you stay awake to pray.

Act of Repentance

P   My brothers and sisters, confess your sins and pray for each other, that you may be healed:

R   I confess to almighty God… *(all pray the confiteor)*

Renewal of Baptismal Promises

If, in the pastoral judgment of the priest, it does not conflict with the celebration at the Easter Vigil, the Renewal of Baptismal Promises may take place now. The people may hold candles lighted from the Easter candle if that is convenient.

P   Through the Paschal mystery, dear friends, we are buried with Christ by baptism into his death, and raised with him to newness of life. I call upon you, therefore, to renew the solemn promises and vows of holy baptism, by which you once renounced Satan and all his works, and promised to serve God faithfully in his holy catholic church.

P   Do you reaffirm your renunciation of evil and renew your commitment to Jesus Christ?

R   I do.

P   Do you believe in God the Father almighty, Creator of heaven and earth?

R   I do.

P   Do you believe in Jesus Christ his only Son our Lord, who was born of the Virgin Mary, was crucified, died, and was buried, rose from the dead, and is now seated at the right hand of the Father?

R   I do.

P   Do you believe in the Holy Spirit, the holy catholic church, the communion of saints, the forgiveness of sins, the resurrection of the body, and life everlasting?

R   I do.

P   Will you continue in the apostles' teaching and fellowship, in the breaking of bread, and in the prayers?

R   I will, with God's help.

P   Will you persevere in resisting evil, and, whenever you fall into sin, repent and return to the Lord?

R   I will, with God's help.

P   Will you proclaim by word and example the Good News of God in Christ?

R   I will, with God's help.

P   Will you seek and serve Christ in all persons, loving your neighbor as yourself?

R   I will, with God's help.

P   Will you strive for justice and peace among all people, and re-
     spect the dignity of every human being?

R   I will, with God's help.

P   Let us now pray to God our Father in the words Christ gave us,
     and ask God for forgiveness and protection from all evil:

All Our Father...

P   Father, giver of life, you know how we can fail despite our reso-
     lution. Accept our repentant prayer and renew in us the grace
     of our baptism.
     We ask this through Christ our Lord.

R   Amen.

Confession

The penitents go to the priests for individual confession.

Final Prayer

Blessed be God the Father of our Lord Jesus Christ, who has blessed
us with all the spiritual blessings of heaven in Christ. Through water
and the Holy Spirit he has delivered us from the death of sin and
raised us to new life in Christ. May we be strengthened to lead the
life worthy of our vocation and preserve the unity of the Spirit by the
peace that binds us together: For there is one Lord, one faith, one
baptism, and one God who is Father of all, over all, through all, and
within all: To him be glory and praise for ever and ever.

R   Amen.

P   May almighty God bless you, the Father, and the Son, ✠ and the
     Holy Spirit.

All Amen.

Recessional Hymn

LENT II

Patrick Rogers, CP

This is a general-purpose penance service whose lines could be used in Lent or Advent, with some adaptation of the readings and hymns to suit the season. My focus is on the details of the ceremony. Photocopy these guidelines and give a copy to each confessor and others directly involved, especially readers, organist, and preacher.

It is a good idea to have a short "briefing" of all the confessors in the sacristy, about 10 minutes before the ceremony begins, indicating how they will be positioned in the church for the confessions, and requesting them to refrain from all unnecessary questioning of the penitents, and from any but the briefest words of counsel and encouragement at that time.

The guidelines could take a form rather like the following:

1. Sacristy

Short prayer for the confessors. A reminder of the format recommended for the individual confessions. (Refrain from unnecessary questioning, etc.)

2. Procession and Hymn

All the confessors, wearing soutane (or habit) and stole, process to sanctuary, genuflect, and remain in sanctuary throughout all of the preparatory phase (i.e. up to confessions).

3. Introductory Greetings and Prayer

The Coordinating Celebrant (CC) uses a standard greeting ("Grace and Peace..."), then invites the people to sit. Briefly explains the value of communal repentance and reconciliation. Asks them to bow their heads for the opening prayer:

Lord, you know me through and through. It is only in your presence that I am fully understood, both in my good points and in my sins. With you there is mercy and fullness of redemption. Give me an honest awareness of what is wrong in my life, and a generous willingness to change whatever needs to be changed. Help me to make up for any harm I have caused to others; and forgive all my offenses against you, most loving Lord.

4. Liturgy of the Word

Scripture, as at Mass:
First Reading, e.g. Isaiah Chapter 1 (Red as scarlet/white as snow)
Responsorial (sung?) Psalm
Gospel
Preacher: Sermon on the welcome God has for all who turn to God

5. Examination of Conscience

May be done in alteration between two or more priests (e.g. the preacher and the CC) in a prayerful form.

Points for the Examination of Conscience
Lord, you search my heart and know me through and through. Help me to recognize the areas in which I have sinned. Have I ...

> *Reverence*
> —loved you, with all my heart and soul?
> inquired about your holy will in my regard?
> tried to keep your commandments?
> —been unfaithful to personal prayer each day?
> and to Sunday Mass?
> —received Eucharist frequently, with faith and devotion?
> —honored your blessed name?
> refrained from swearing, blasphemy, indecent language?
> taken your name in vain?
> —trusted fully in you, at all times?
>
> *Justice*
> —shown kindness, respect, and understanding toward my neighbor?
> —given a fair day's work for a fair day's pay? (and vice versa).

—stolen or damaged goods belonging to another?
—withheld payment of my lawful debts including taxes?
—made false claims, for things I had no right to get?
—been reckless about the life and safety of other people?
—taken or distributed drugs that are injurious to health?
—threatened the livelihood of others, by unfair practices?
—driven, or been abusive, while under the influence of alcohol?
—taken the character of others, by detraction or plain slander?
—neglected to help the poor and needy, from what I could spare?
—taken care of my own family according to my state in life?
—exploited sexuality (my own or another's)?

Family
—been loyal and faithful in my family life?
—treated my partner (or fiancé) with proper respect and love?
—avoided fornication, adultery, loose behavior, immoral books and TV?
—shared my income honestly and openly with my family?
—taken a proper, active interest in my children's education?
—spent time with them? let them see that I love them?
—explained right and wrong to them, according to their age?
—given them good example, by my own attitudes and actions?
—supported other people's family life, by encouragement and sympathy?
—tried to observe the kind of purity proper to my state in life?

Lord, if I have committed serious sin in any of these areas, let me have the courage to admit it honestly and repent of it from my heart. May the light of your truth shine on my mind, and the warmth of your peace be in my heart.

6. General Confession of Sins

Confiteor and Act of Contrition
Our Father

7. Guidelines for the Individual Confessions

P   The emphasis is on having the right frame of mind for receiving the mercy of God. It will be enough to say to the priest something like the following: "Father, I am sorry for all my sins, and in particular for... (here you mention any serious sins you are aware of)... and anything else in which I have offended almighty God." The confessor will give you absolution. There is no need to repeat the Act of Contrition, which we have all recited together.

While the individual confessions are heard, the rest of the congregation will join in quiet meditation, with the help of prayers and hymns and silent pauses. Please remain until the end of the ceremony.

Confessors should be at their stations around the church; preferably standing. Other ministers should guide the penitents, so that a short line is formed before each priest (minimum of 12 feet clearance between penitent and line!). Priest might place his hands on the penitent's shoulders as a gesture of welcome, and in this way reassure those who are nervous and afraid.

8. Communal Prayer Penance

All the confessors return to sanctuary where the CC leads a prayer of penance, common to all. This could be the En Ego or Saint Francis of Assisi's Prayer for Peace, etc.

LENT III

Bill Murphy

Hymn

Sign of the Cross

Greeting

P   Grace, mercy, and peace be with you
from God the Father
and from Jesus Christ
who loved us
and gave his life for us.

R   And also with you.

Introduction

On behalf of the priests of the parish, I welcome you all to our parish celebration of penance and God's forgiveness.

Our celebration of penance is not an isolated happening. It is part of our lenten journey toward conversion during which we try to turn away from the darkness of sin and evil and come back to our God, the God of light and love. All this is, of course, our preparation for Easter, the greatest feast in the Christian calendar when we will celebrate the resurrection of Jesus Christ, who is the light of the world.

At this stage in our lenten preparation we come together:
—to confess and to celebrate the love and forgiveness of God;
—to acknowledge and to confess our own weakness, our frequent failures, our sins, which have placed obstacles between ourselves and God and barriers between ourselves and others;
—and to confess our need and to ask for God's love, forgiveness, and healing.

Let us now pause for a moment and ask the Father for that wisdom of the Spirit that alone can help us to realize and appreciate God's love and forgiveness and enable us to recognize, acknowledge, and repent of the shortcomings, the failures, and the sins in our lives.

Prayer

P   Let us pray.
     God our Father,
     You are compassion and love,
     slow to anger and rich in mercy.
     In your great tenderness wipe away our sins.
     Create a clean heart in us.
     Put into us a new and constant spirit,
     the Spirit of your Son Jesus Christ, Our Lord.

R   Amen.

First Reading   Isaiah 1:11, 15–18

A reading from the prophet Isaiah.

"What are your endless sacrifices to me?
says Yahweh.
I am sick of holocausts of rams
and the fat of calves.
The blood of bulls and of goats revolts me.
When you stretch out your hands
I turn my eyes away.
You may multiply your prayers,
I shall not listen.
Your hands are covered with blood,
wash, make yourselves clean.

"Take your wrongdoing out of my sight.
Cease to do evil.
Learn to do good,
search for justice,

36

help the oppressed,
be just to the orphan,
plead for the widow.

"Come now, let us talk this over,
says Yahweh.
Though your sins are like scarlet,
they shall be as white as snow;
though they are red as crimson,
they shall be like wool."

The word of the Lord.

R   Thanks be to God.

Responsorial Psalm   Psalm 51

R   Have mercy on me, O God, in your goodness.

1.   Have mercy on me, O God, in your goodness.
     in your great tenderness wipe away my faults;
     wash me clean of my guilt
     purify me from my sin. R

2.   For I am well aware of my faults,
     I have my sin constantly in mind,
     having sinned against none other than you,
     having done what you regard as wrong. R

3.   God, create a clean heart in me,
     put into me a new and constant spirit,
     do not banish me from your presence,
     do not deprive me of your holy spirit. R

4.   Save me from death, God my savior,
     and my tongue will proclaim your righteousness;
     Lord, open my lips,
     and my mouth will speak out your praise. R

Acclamation

Glory to you, O Christ, you are the Word of God.
A pure heart create for me, O God,
and give me again the joy of your help.
Glory to you, O Christ, you are the Word of God.

Gospel   Mark 12:28–34

A reading from the holy Gospel according to Mark.

One of the scribes who had listened to them debating and had observed how well Jesus had answered them, now came up and put a
question to him, "Which is the first of all the commandments?" Jesus
replied, "This is the first: *Listen, Israel, the Lord our God is the one Lord,
and you must love the Lord your God with all your heart, with all your
soul*, with all your mind and *with all your strength*. The second is this:
You must love your neighbor as yourself. There is no commandment
greater than these." The scribe said to him, "Well spoken, Master;
what you have said is true: that he is one and there is no other. To
love him with all your heart, with all your understanding and
strength, and to love your neighbor as yourself, this is far more important than any holocaust or sacrifice." Jesus, seeing how wisely he
had spoken, said, "You are not far from the kingdom of God."

The gospel of the Lord.

R   Praise to you, Lord Jesus Christ.

Suggestions for Homily

We are here tonight to experience God's forgiving, healing, reconciling love in the sacrament of penance and to celebrate it together in
this communal act of prayer and worship.

The fact that we are here is a sign that we have some awareness that
we are sinners, that all is not well in our lives, that we have all fallen
short of what God wants us to be, that we have missed the target.
The fact that we are here is also a sign that we want to do something
about it, that we want to turn away from sin and come back to God.

"To err is human, to forgive is divine." We know how difficult it is to forgive when a wrong has been done to us. Knowing how difficult it is to forgive, we are slow to ask forgiveness from someone we have wronged. We must be careful not to adopt this attitude toward God. The greatest sin of all is to doubt or question God's love and free-flowing forgiveness after all God has said and done to prove it.

> Come back to me with all your heart,
> for I am all tenderness and compassion.

Why should we doubt God's tenderness, compassion, and readiness to forgive, when human beings, creatures of God, are so often capable of remarkable tenderness, compassion, and readiness to forgive? Perhaps you can recall some occasion when you were forgiven unconditionally by another—a parent, a spouse, a friend. Perhaps on some occasion you have silently forgiven someone who hurt you deeply, even when you knew that you would get no thanks for it and that your silent forgiveness would be just taken for granted. Again and again we have seen people who forgave men of violence who killed a loved one or caused serious injury to themselves. The supreme example of forgiveness was that of Jesus on the cross when he spoke the words: "Father, forgive them, for they know not what they are doing." That is what God's forgiveness is like, for Jesus is God in action. In the sacrament of penance we meet our forgiving God. We receive the same forgiveness.

But our sin is not simply a matter between ourselves and God; it affects others, too. Each of us is a unique individual, but each of us is also made for life with others. According to an old saying, people live in the shadow of one another. Our lives are intertwined with the lives of others. We bear one another along through life. We are responsible for one another. Sometimes we support one another, sometimes we fail one another or undermine one another. We edify or scandalize one another. We inspire or dishearten one another. We bring people closer to God and to others or we place obstacles and barriers in their way to God and to others—by what we do and by what we fail to do.

We come together tonight not as individuals so much as a group of Christians who want:

— to confess and celebrate God's love for us, God's people, and God's forgiveness;

— to confess the ways and times we failed God and failed one another;

— to ask God to grant us forgiveness.

As we celebrate the sacrament of penance tonight not as individuals but as a group, we ask you to please stay until the end so that we may all thank God together.

Examination of Conscience

You must love the Lord your God with all your heart ...

How do I think of God? An almighty power I must placate?

A severe judge who might condemn me to Hell?

A stickler for rules? Or as my loving, heavenly Father?

Am I open to God's presence in my life?

Do I listen carefully to God's word in the Bible?

How important is the Eucharist in my life?

Do I really want God to direct my life?

Do I spend time in quiet prayer seeking God's will for me?

Am I too concerned with myself, my own interests, my own inclinations and desires, and do these crowd God out?

You must love your neighbor as yourself...

Do I only love people who are nice to me? Does my love have to be earned?

Do I take more trouble with "important" people than with "ordinary" people?

Is there anyone whom I do not wish well? Anyone of whom I am jealous? Anyone whom I do not forgive?

Do I treat my family with love and care?

Do I love and respect enough my wife, my husband, my children, my parents?

Am I concerned about other people, especially those less fortunate than myself?

Am I thoughtless? Am I selfish? Am I proud?

Do I speak out on behalf of the needy?

Do I share what I have with them?
Do I respect other people's property?
Am I truthful and honest in my dealings with others?
Do I judge others? Do I spread gossip about others?
Am I inclined to blame others when something goes wrong?
Do I sin against purity in mind or action?
Am I a committed follower of Jesus Christ?

Confiteor

All   I confess …*(all pray the confiteor)*

Act of Sorrow

All   O my God…

P   God our Father, forgive our sins.
We ask this as your Son Jesus taught us to ask:

All   Our Father…

P   As a sign of our willingness to be reconciled, let us offer one another a sign of peace.

Individual Confession and Absolution

Prayers/hymns/decades of the Rosary/periods of silence during confessions.

Prayer of Thanksgiving
after confessors return to sanctuary

Let us pray.
God our Father,
You sent your Son
to reconcile the world to yourself.
Grant that by walking the path of prayer,
penance, and justice,
we may become more visibly like Christ
and more worthy to celebrate his death and resurrection.
We ask this through Christ our Lord.

Final Blessing

P   The Lord be with you.

R   And also with you.

The solemn blessing for Ordinary Time IV, from the sacramentary, would work well here.

P   May almighty God bless you, the Father, and the Son, ✠ and the Holy Spirit.

R   Amen.

P   Go in peace to love and serve the Lord.

R   Thanks be to God.

Final Hymn

HOLY WEEK

Michael Doherty

Introduction

P   In the name of the Father, and of the Son, and of the Holy Spirit.

R   Amen.

P   The Lord be with you.

R   And also with you.

P   Among those who cheered on Palm Sunday were some who mocked on Good Friday. The streets that welcomed Jesus became the roads of rejection. If we are people who smile at Jesus at Sunday Mass but mock or reject him during the week by our thoughts, words, deeds, or omissions, we need forgiveness. This week we will follow Christ through death to new life; our penitential service and sacrament of reconciliation can help us die to sin and rise to the new life to which Christ invites us.

Opening Prayer

P   Let us pray.
God our Father,
Your Word, Jesus Christ, spoke to a sinful world and brought humankind the gift of reconciliation by the suffering and death he endured. Teach us, the people who bear his name, to follow the example he gave us: May our faith, hope, and charity turn hatred to love, conflict to peace, death to eternal life.
We ask this through Christ our Lord.

R   Amen.

Reading   Mark 14:32–42

A reading form the holy Gospel according to Mark.

They came to a small estate called Gethsemane, and Jesus said to his disciples, "Stay here while I pray." Then he took Peter and James and John with him. And a sudden fear came over him, and great distress. And he said to them, "My soul is sorrowful to the point of death. Wait here, and keep awake." And going on a little further he threw himself on the ground and prayed that, if it were possible, this hour might pass him by. "Abba (Father)!" he said. "Everything is possible for you. Take this cup away from me. But let it be as you, not I, would have it." He came back and found them sleeping, and he said to Peter, "Simon, are you asleep? Had you not the strength to keep awake one hour? You should be awake, and praying not to be put to the test. The spirit is willing, but the flesh is weak." Again he went away and prayed, saying the same words. And once more he came back and found them sleeping, their eyes were so heavy; and they could find no answer for him. He came back a third time and said to them, "You can sleep on now and take your rest. It is all over. The hour has come. Now the Son of Man is to be betrayed into the hands of sinners. Get up! Let us go! My betrayer is close at hand already."

The gospel of the Lord.

R   Praise to you, Lord Jesus Christ.

Examination of Conscience

1.   To seek peace and reconciliation, we must first become aware of our sinfulness.
2.   "Watch and pray" was what the Lord asked his followers to do.
3.   In silence, we will consider various aspects of our lives and consider how watchful or prayerful we have been:
      in our relationship with God
      at home and at work
      in our respect for ourselves and others, for their lives, their
        dignity, their bodies, their possessions
      in our use of alcohol
      in what we have failed to do.

Short period of quiet reflection

The Confiteor

P   Let us acknowledge our sinfulness and ask for God's merciful forgiveness:

All   I confess ...*(all pray the confiteor)*

Litany

In his great love, Christ willingly suffered and died for our sins and for the sins of all humankind. Let us come before him in faith and hope to pray for the salvation of the world.

R   Christ, graciously hear us.

Healer of body and soul, bind up the wounds of our hearts, that our lives may grow strong through grace. R

Help us to strip ourselves of sin and put on the new life of grace. R

Redeemer of the world, give us the spirit of penance and a deeper devotion to your passion, so that we may have a fuller share in your risen glory. R

You promised paradise to the good thief, take us with you into your kingdom. R

You died for us and rose again; make us share in your death and resurrection. R

P   Now, in obedience to Christ himself, let us join in prayer to the Father, asking him to forgive us as we forgive others:

All   Our Father ...

Individual confession follows

Praise of God's Mercy

R   Great is God's love, love without end.

      O give thanks to the Lord for the Lord is good. R

Give thanks to the God of gods. R
Give thanks to the Lord of lords. R

Who alone has wrought marvelous works. R
Whose wisdom it was made the skies. R
Who fixed the earth firmly on the seas. R

It was God who made the great lights. R
The sun to rule in the day. R
The moon and the stars in the night. R

P   Let us pray.
We thank you, Father, for giving us new life through the death
and resurrection of your Son. By the power of the Holy Spirit,
may we show to the world the love and forgiveness his risen
life has brought us.
We ask this through Christ our Lord.

R   Amen.

ALL SAINTS/ALL SOULS

Oliver Crilly

Entrance Song

Greeting

P   In the name of the Father, and of the Son, and of the Holy Spirit.

R   Amen.

P   The Lord be with you.

R   And also with you.

Introduction

Every time we pray, we join in with the prayer of the whole church—not just on earth, but of the whole communion of saints. They welcome us and embrace us and bring us close to God.

Let us feel embraced by all our saints during this penitential service as they help us, through God's grace, to come closer to one another and to God's forgiving love.

Opening Prayer

P   Let us pray.
God, our Father, we gather before you in our weakness and sin-fulness, repentant and sorrowful for our sins, for what we have done and failed to do. But we gather also in hope, because we gather as your people, united in the church and in the commun-ion of saints. We ask you to cleanse and renew us, and as you in your mercy forgive us, we ask you to help us, through the power of your Holy Spirit, to forgive one another. Grant this through Christ our Lord.

R   Amen.

LITURGY OF THE WORD

First Reading   Romans 6:2–14

Consider yourselves dead to sin but alive to God.

A reading from the letter of Paul to the Romans.

We are dead to sin, so how can we continue to live in it? You have been taught that when we were baptized in Christ Jesus we were baptized in his death; in other words, when we were baptized we went into the tomb with him and joined him in death, so that as Christ was raised from the dead by the Father's glory, we too might live a new life.

If in union with Christ we have imitated his death, we shall also imitate him in his resurrection. We must realize that our former selves have been crucified with him to destroy this sinful body and to free us from the slavery of sin. When a man dies, of course, he has finished with sin.

But we believe that having died with Christ we shall return to life with him: Christ, as we know, having been raised from the dead will never die again. Death has no power over him any more. When he died, he died, once for all, to sin, so his life now is life with God and in that way, you too must consider yourselves to be dead to sin but alive for God in Christ Jesus.

That is why you must not let sin reign in your mortal bodies or command your obedience to bodily passions, why you must not let any part of your body turn into an unholy weapon fighting on the side of sin; you should, instead, offer yourselves to God, and consider yourselves dead men brought back to life; you should make every part of your body into a weapon fighting on the side of God; and then sin will no longer dominate your life, since you are living by grace and not by law.

The word of the Lord.

R   Thanks be to God.

Responsorial Psalm

Psalm 32:1–7

R   Lord, forgive the wrong I have done.

1.   Happy the man whose fault is forgiven,
whose sin is blotted out;
happy the man whom Yahweh
accuses of no guilt,
whose spirit is incapable of deceit! R

2.   All the time I kept silent, my bones were wasting away
with groans, day in, day out;
day and night your hand
lay heavy on me;
my heart grew parched as stubble
in summer drought. R

3.   At last I admitted to you I had sinned;
no longer concealing my guilt,
I said, "I will go to Yahweh
and confess my fault."
And you, you have forgiven the wrong I did,
have pardoned my sin. R

4.   That is why each of your servants prays to you
in time of trouble;
even if floods come rushing down,
they will never reach him.
You are a hiding place for me,
you guard me when in trouble,
you surround me with songs of deliverance. R

Gospel Acclamation

John 8:12

Alleluia! Alleluia!
I am the light of the world.
Anyone who follows me
will have the light of life.
Alleluia!

Gospel   Matthew 4:12–17

Repent, for the kingdom of heaven is close at hand.

A reading from the holy Gospel according to Matthew.

Hearing that John had been arrested, he went back to Galilee, and leaving Nazareth he went and settled in Capernaum, a lakeside town on the borders of Zebulun and Naphtali. In this way the prophecy of Isaiah was to be fulfilled:

> *Land of Zebulun! Land of Naphtali!*
> *Way of the sea on the far side of Jordan,*
> *Galilee of the nations!*
> *The people that lived in darkness*
> *has seen a great light;*
> *on those who dwell in the land and shadow of death*
> *a light has dawned.*

From that moment Jesus began his preaching with the message, "Repent, for the kingdom of heaven is close at hand."

The gospel of the Lord.

R   Praise to you, Lord Jesus Christ.

Suggestions for Homily

If we think of saints only as those very famous people who have been canonized by the church, we are missing something. Because we all have our own saints—all those in our own family and in our own parish who "have gone before us in the sign of faith." These are all the women and men, girls and boys, married, single, religious, priests, and even babies who have died and make up that part of the family of God who are in heaven or in purgatory.

The people of God on earth are sometimes called the faithful, and those who have gone before us are called the faithful departed. It's a good description; because our people who have gone before us—our own saints—have been faithful to us. That applies in a special way to parents and grandparents, uncles and aunts, teachers, religious, and priests who have taught us and influenced us. All our saints not only *have* been faithful to us, but continue to be faithful to us.

It's not just that we pray for them—they pray for us and are near us in the love of God. Can you imagine our saints praying for us, saying "May they have rest and peace, and may the light of God's love shine on them"?

It is sin that disturbs the peace of our lives, of our minds and hearts, and it is sin that blocks out the light of God's loving presence and makes us forget about God. When we think of our faithful people praying for us, we can be sure that their greatest desire is that we should be close to God, and through being close to God that we be close to them, too. As we celebrate this penitential rite, let us be lifted up in the arms of all our saints into the presence of God our Father who loves us and forgives us and wants us to be fully and whole-heartedly reconciled with God and with each other. We need not be afraid, because forgiveness is only a request away.

Examination of Conscience
Some time should be given now for an examination of conscience. After a period of silence, some guidelines for the examination of conscience may be given if it is considered helpful.

P   The Lord is merciful. The Lord makes us clean of heart and leads us out into freedom when we acknowledge our guilt. Let us ask the Lord to forgive us and bind up the wounds inflicted by our sins.

All   I confess to almighty God... *(all pray the confiteor)*

P   Let us now pray to God our Father in the words Christ gave us, and ask God for forgiveness and protection from all evil.

All   Our Father...

The priest concludes:
Lord, through the intercession of all the saints,
help us to confess our sins
and grant us your forgiveness.
May the souls of the faithful departed rest in peace.
We ask this through Christ our Lord.

R   Amen.

Individual confession and absolution follow now.

After the individual confessions are completed, or at an arranged time, the chief celebrant returns to the sanctuary and addresses some words to the people, encouraging them to be thankful for the grace of repentance and forgiveness, and urging them to carry out their firm purpose of amending their lives.

The Magnificat

R   The Lord has remembered his mercy.

1.   My soul proclaims the greatness of the Lord,
       and my spirit *exults in God my savior;*
       because *he has looked upon his lowly handmaid.*
       Yes, from this day forward all generations will call me blessed.
       R

2.   For the Almighty has done great things for me.
       Holy is his name,
       and *his mercy reaches from age to age for those who fear him.* R

3.   He has shown the power of his arm,
       he has routed the proud of heart.
       He has pulled down princes from their thrones *and exalted the lowly.* R

4.   *The hungry he has filled with good things,* the rich sent empty
       away. R

5.   *He has come to the help of Israel his servant, mindful of his mercy*
       —according to the promise he made to our ancestors—
       of his mercy to Abraham and to his descendants forever. R

Prayer of Thanksgiving

P   God our Father,
       we thank you for this experience of common prayer,
       of listening to your word,
       and especially of your love and forgiveness.
       We ask you to grant us the grace of perseverance,
       that we may serve you faithfully from now on
       in our earthly lives,

and one day be united with all your saints
in your heavenly kingdom.
We ask this through Christ our Lord.

R   Amen.

The Blessing

Then the priest blesses all present:
May the Lord guide your hearts in the way of love and fill you with
Christ-like patience.

R   Amen.

May the Lord give you strength to walk in newness of life and to
please the Lord in all things.

R   Amen.

May almighty God bless you, the Father, and the Son, ✠ and the
Holy Spirit.

R   Amen.

The Dismissal

The Lord has freed you from your sins. Go in peace.

R   Thanks be to God.

ON FEASTS OF OUR LADY

Oliver Crilly

This short service is intended for use on the occasion of feasts of Our Lady, such as on the day before the feast, or during a novena of preparation.

Introduction

P   In the name of the Father, and of the Son, and of the Holy Spirit.

R   Amen.

P   The Lord be with you.

R   And also with you.

The priest should set the scene briefly.

Opening Prayer

P   Let us pray.
    Lord Jesus, at the moment of your death on the cross for our sins, you gave us your mother Mary to be our mother and mother of the church. Help us to approach her with confidence as the refuge of sinners, and to learn from her how to be true disciples—open to your Spirit in our daily lives. Help us to be open to your healing presence, to your healing and forgiving love.
    We ask this through Christ our Lord.

R   Amen.

Reading   Luke 1:26–38

A reading from the holy Gospel according to Luke.

In the sixth month, the angel Gabriel was sent by God to a town in Galilee called Nazareth, to a virgin betrothed to a man named Joseph, of the house of David; and the virgin's name was Mary. He went in and said to her, "Rejoice, so highly favored! The Lord is with you." She was deeply disturbed by these words and asked herself what this greeting could mean, but the angel said to her, "Mary, do not be afraid; you have won God's favor. Listen! You are to conceive and bear a son, and you must name him Jesus. He will be great and will be called Son of the Most High. The Lord God will give him the throne of his ancestor David; he will rule over the House of Jacob for ever and his reign will have no end." Mary said to the angel, "But how can this come about, since I am a virgin?" "The Holy Spirit will come upon you," the angel answered, "and the power of the Most High will cover you with its shadow. And so the child will be holy and will be called Son of God. Know this too: your kinswoman Elizabeth has, in her old age, herself conceived a son, and she whom people called barren is now in her sixth month, *for nothing is impossible to God.*" "I am the handmaid of the Lord," said Mary, "let what you have said be done to me." And the angel left her.

The gospel of the Lord.

R   Praise to you Lord Jesus Christ.

Examination of Conscience

A quiet time is allowed for examination of conscience, with a special emphasis on our lack of expectations and on our need for openness to the work of the Spirit in our lives.

The best way to honor Mary is to imitate her;
The qualities of Mary in the story of the Annunciation are:
> *1. Openness —"I am the handmaid of the Lord, let what you have said be done to me."*
> *2. Practical searching to understand how God's will is to be realized in the concrete circumstances of her life —"How can this come about?"*
Am I closed to God's will in my life? Have I lost my sense of wonder and expectation? Have I lost hope?

The Confiteor

P   Let us acknowledge our sinfulness, our lack of openness and expectation, and seek God's forgiveness:

A   I confess to almighty God...*(all pray the confiteor)*

Litany

Leader: Jesus, eternal truth, you give us true freedom.

A   Lord Jesus, be our salvation.

L   Jesus, you are the way to the Father.

A   Lord Jesus, be our salvation.

L   Jesus, you are the resurrection and the life; those who believe in you, even if they are dead, will live.

A   Lord Jesus, be our salvation.

Our Father

P   Now, in obedience to Christ himself, let us pray together to our loving and forgiving Father:

A   Our Father...

Individual Confession

Individual confession follows. When all or most of the penitents have been to confession, this concluding prayer of thanksgiving is said:

P   Let us pray.
We thank you, Father, God of compassion and mercy. May we who have experienced your faithful love and your faithful forgiveness be reconciled with one another, and may we go forth to show your love and compassion to everyone we meet. We ask this through Christ our Lord.

A   Amen.

PARISH CELEBRATION I

Oliver Crilly

Theme: The Beatitudes

Opening Hymn and Enthronement of the Book

During the opening hymn, the presider, readers, homilist, confessors, and servers process with the lectionary and solemnly enthrone it on the lectern, where it is incensed by the presider.

Greeting

P   May God our Father and the Lord Jesus Christ give you grace and peace.

R   Amen.

Opening Prayer

God our Father,
you so loved the world that you sent your only Son
for our salvation.
Help us now,
as we hear again the word of that same Jesus Christ,
to acknowledge our failure to follow him,
and humbly to ask your forgiveness.
We ask this through Jesus the Lord.

R   Amen.

LITURGY OF THE WORD

First Reading   1 John 1:9–10; 2:1–2

A reading from the first letter of John.

If we acknowledge our sins,
then God who is faithful and just
will forgive our sins and purify us

---

from everything that is wrong.
To say that we have never sinned
is to call God a liar
and to show that his word in not in us.

I am writing this, my children,
to stop you sinning;
but if anyone should sin,
we have our advocate with the Father,
Jesus Christ, who is just;
he is the sacrifice that takes our sins away,
and not only ours,
but the whole world's.

The word of the Lord.

R   Thanks be to God.

A brief period of silence, for personal reflection, follows the reading.

Responsorial Psalm   Psalm 25:4–5, 8–11

R   Turn to me, Lord, and have mercy.

1.   Yahweh, make your ways known to me,
       teach me your paths.
       Set me in the way of your truth, and teach me,
       for you are the God who saves me. R

2.   Yahweh is so good, so upright,
       he teaches the way to sinners;
       in all that is right he guides the humble,
       and instructs the poor in his way. R

3.   All Yahweh's paths are love and truth
       for those who keep his covenant and his decrees.
       For the sake of your name, Yahweh,
       forgive my guilt for it is great. R

Gospel Reading   Matthew 5:1–10

Happy are the poor in spirit, for theirs is the kingdom of heaven.

A reading from the holy Gospel according to Matthew.

Seeing the crowds, Jesus went up the hill. There he sat down and was joined by his disciples. Then he began to speak. This is what he taught them:

"How happy are the poor in spirit:
theirs is the kingdom of heaven.
Happy *the gentle:*
they shall have the earth for their heritage.
Happy those who mourn:
they shall be comforted.
Happy those who hunger and thirst for what is right:
they shall be satisfied.
Happy the merciful:
they shall have mercy shown them.
Happy the pure in heart:
they shall see God.
Happy the peacemakers:
they shall be called sons of God.
Happy those who are persecuted in the cause of right:
theirs is the kingdom of heaven.

The gospel of the Lord.

R   Praise to you, Lord Jesus Christ.

Homily
The homily leads on to an examination of conscience and is followed by a period of silence for personal recollection.

THE SACRAMENT OF PENANCE

P   My brothers and sisters, confess your sins and pray for each other, that you may be healed.

All   I confess to almighty God...*(all pray the confiteor)*

P   The Lord is merciful. The Lord makes us clean of heart and leads us out into freedom when we acknowledge our guilt. Let us ask God to forgive us and bind up the wounds inflicted by our sins. Let us now pray to God our Father in the words Christ gave us, and ask God for forgiveness and protection from all evil.

All   Our Father...

P   Lord, draw near to your servants who, in the presence of your church, confess that they are sinners. Through the ministry of the church free them from all sin so that, renewed in spirit, they may give you thankful praise.
We ask this through Christ our Lord.

R   Amen.

Sign of Peace
P   As brothers and sisters who reconcile themselves before their Father, let us offer each other a sign of peace.

Individual Confession
Reflective music may be played during confessions. Enough priests should be on hand to conclude the service in a reasonable time, but, if the numbers are very large, the final prayer and blessing may be said after a fixed period, with confessions continuing afterward for the rest of the congregation.

Final Prayer
Almighty and merciful God
we thank you for your faithful love
and your faithful forgiveness.
We ask you to help us to show in our lives
the compassion and forgiveness that you show us.
We make this prayer through Jesus the Lord.

R   Amen.

Final Blessing

P   Bow your heads and pray for God's blessing.

     May almighty God keep you from all harm and bless you with every good gift.

R   Amen.

P   May God set God's word in your heart and fill you with lasting joy.

R   Amen.

P   May you walk in God's ways always knowing what is right and good, until you enter your heavenly inheritance.

R   Amen.

P   May almighty God bless you, the Father, and the Son, ✠ and the Holy Spirit.

R   Amen.

PARISH CELEBRATION II

Patrick Jones

Theme: God's judging and saving word

The book of God's word is carried in procession and becomes a focus of attention. The Gospel sayings used in the examination of conscience could be displayed on banners or slides.

INTRODUCTORY RITES

Song
Sing a song expressing our worship or repentance, such as, "God of Mercy and Compassion," or a seasonal song, such as "O Come Emmanuel."

Greeting and Introduction

P   In the name of the Father, and of the Son, and of the Holy Spirit.
R   Amen.

P   May the grace, mercy, and peace of God our Father and of Christ Jesus our Lord be with you.

   Tonight we gather for a service of repentance and, as we begin, we place the book of Gospels in our midst. Let it dominate our gathering. Let it give us direction.

The book of Gospels or lectionary is placed on the ambo.

P   We will listen to God's word. We will allow ourselves to be judged by God's word. But it is also a saving word, proclaiming God's mercy for all of us.

   Tonight, we have come together to accept Jesus at his word: He comes to save. We gather in common prayer—asking God to show mercy to us—and then, realizing that such prayer is always answered, proclaiming our praise of God's mercy.

God's ways of mercy are without limitation. What we do tonight, celebrating the sacrament of penance, is one of them.

We must not feel in any way pressured to act in a strange way—rather, we should remember the mercy of God—that it touches each of us—it provides the occasion to celebrate the sacrament of mercy—quietly, briefly, without fuss—as a prayer—expressing our sorrow for sin and receiving pardon and peace. Because we are engaged in common prayer, please remain until the end, so that we can thank God together.

Let us pray.
God our Father, you love us. Through our sins we have drifted away from you. Help us to respond to your loving invitation to return. Grant to us a heart renewed. Recreate in us your own Spirit. We ask this through Jesus the Lord.

R   Amen.

LITURGY OF THE WORD

Reading   Hebrews 4:12–13

The word of God, like a two-edged sword, judges us and saves us.

A reading from the letter to the Hebrews.

The word of God is something alive and active: it cuts like any double-edged sword but more finely: it can slip through the place where the soul is divided from the spirit, or joints from the marrow; it can judge the secret emotions and thoughts. No created thing can hide from him; everything is uncovered and open to the eyes of the one to whom we must give account of ourselves.

The word of the Lord.

R   Thanks be to God.

Psalm

e.g. "Grant to us, O Lord"

Gospel   Luke 15:11–32

Is it possible to have a renewed heart? Jesus assures us that our Father in heaven will answer and welcome us.

A reading from the holy Gospel according to Luke.

Jesus also said, "A man had two sons. The younger said to his father, 'Father, let me have the share of the estate that would come to me.' So the father divided the property between them. A few days later the younger son got together everything he had and left for a distant country where he squandered his money on a life of debauchery.

"When he had spent it all, that country experienced a severe famine, and now he began to feel the pinch, so he hired himself out to one of the local inhabitants who put him on his farm to feed the pigs. And he would willingly have filled his belly with the husks the pigs were eating but no one offered him anything. Then he came to his senses and said, 'How many of my father's paid servants have more food than they want, and here I am dying of hunger! I will leave this place and go to my father and say: Father, I have sinned against heaven and against you; I no longer deserve to be called your son; treat me as one of your paid servants.' So he left the place and went back to his father.

"While he was still a long way off, his father saw him and was moved with pity. He ran to the boy, clasped him in his arms and kissed him tenderly. Then his son said, 'Father, I have sinned against heaven and against you. I no longer deserve to be called your son.' But the father said to his servants, 'Quick! Bring out the best robe and put it on him; put a ring on his finger and sandals on his feet. Bring the calf we have been fattening, and kill it; we are going to have a feast, a celebration, because this son of mine was dead and has come back to life; he was lost and is found.' And they began to celebrate.

"Now the elder son was out in the fields, and on his way back, as he drew near the house, he could hear music and dancing. Calling one of the servants he asked what it was all about. 'Your brother has come,' replied the servant, 'and your father has killed the calf we had fattened because he has got him back safe and sound.' He was angry then and refused to go in, and his father came out to plead with him; but he answered his father, 'Look, all these years I have slaved for you and never once disobeyed your orders, yet you never offered me so much as a kid for me to celebrate with my friends. But, for this son of yours, when he comes back after swallowing up your property—he and his women—you kill the calf we had been fattening.'

"The father said, 'My son, you are with me always and all I have is yours. But it was only right we should celebrate and rejoice, because your brother here was dead and has come to life; he was lost and is found.'"

The gospel of the Lord.

R   Praise to you, Lord Jesus Christ.

Suggestions for Homily

1. We have heard the story of the prodigal son so often—probably the best story in the Bible.

We know it is a parable—and that the important thing about a parable is its message or moral. And we know the moral—God is like the forgiving father. He accepts the sinner, like the father accepted the prodigal son.

2. We know all this so well that we run the danger of underplaying it.

We make great claims about God because of this parable—God is, above all, a God of forgiveness—God's forgiveness is without limit. God remains, always and simply, a forgiving God. Now let us capture the atmosphere of the story—the atmosphere of forgiveness and reconciliation. We have it here. As a people, we are sinful. It is worth acknowledging this because we know that there is a great welcome for the sinner. God is comfortable in the presence of sinners. God rushes out to meet the sinner.

It is worth examining our consciences, our lives. The sinner has something to say. Open your heart like the son, realize your sinfulness. Of course, God knows it all—even better than we know ourselves. The father did not have to listen to the son's prepared speech. He wanted his son home.

The father does not even get as far as saying to the son that he should behave himself in the future.

And that's the moral of the story—God wants to do likewise with us.

We are faced with a God who has mercy without limit. Yes, we are talking about a limitless gift of grace. We are celebrating the gift among us.

3. Ask. Accept.

Place your sinfulness before God. There is no older brother questioning, angry, unforgiving. There is only a forgiving Father. The focus of attention is not on us—or our sins—but on the love and mercy of God.

There is only a God who is the Father of mercies, who through the death and resurrection of his Son, Jesus, has reconciled the world to himself and sent the Holy Spirit among us for the forgiveness of our sins.

4. The only difficulty that can exist is on our part. The forgiving Father is prepared to rush out and embrace us. All we need to do is to move in his direction.

Examination of Conscience
It is best that the following be spoken by a number of people.

Let us examine our lives and assess our living in the light of the Gospel. God's word will prompt us, jolt us, judge us, and save us. We will realize the sinfulness of our lives and accept God's mercy and forgiveness.

1. Jesus said, "Repent, for the kingdom of heaven is close at hand" (Matthew 4:17).
    Is there serious sin in my life?

Since my last confession, have I made a real effort to improve?
Have I lived at peace with God? with others?

2. Jesus said, "You must love the Lord your God with all your Heart,
with all your soul, and with all your mind" (Matthew 22:37).
Do I love God with all my heart? Is there any other god—self
success, pleasure, wealth—that comes before God?
Do I try to pray each day?
Do I respect and reverence God's name? Am I faithful to Sunday Mass?

3. Jesus said,"I give you a new commandment: love one another"
(John 13:34).
Have I tried to love my neighbor as myself?
Have I helped those in need? Have I been aware of their needs?
Have I remembered the sick, the deprived, those whom we put
on the margins of our society?
Have I been a faithful and loving member of my family?
Have I contributed to building a happy home and family? Have
I loved and honored my parents?
Have I sinned against chastity?

4. Jesus said, "Happy those who hunger and thirst for what is right:
they shall be satisfied" (Matthew 5:6).
Am I selfish, self-seeking, caring only for my own wants and
needs? Have I respected the rights of others?
Do I pay fair wages and provide proper working conditions?
Do I overcharge? make false claims?
Am I guilty of stealing? Have I stolen or damaged other peo
ple's property? Do I respect public property?
Do I respect life? Am I conscious of other people's safety?
Have I lied in a serious way?

5. Jesus said, "Peace I bequeath to you, my own peace I give you"
(John 14:27).
Am I a person of peace? Do I support, condone, encourage violence in any form? Have I been violent, in word or action? Am I
a source of trouble or discontent at home, at work?

6. Jesus said, "You are the salt of the earth..., the light of the world." (Matthew 5:13-14).

Am I willing to be counted as a Christian?

7. Jesus said, "Courage, your sins are forgiven" (Matthew 9:2).

LITURGY OF RECONCILIATION

General Confession of Sins

Lord Jesus, you forgive us our sins. Lord, have mercy.

Lord Jesus, you bring peace to our world. Lord, have mercy.

Lord Jesus, you embrace us in friendship. Lord, have mercy.

Lord Jesus, you promise us life. Lord, have mercy.

Lord Jesus, you welcome us home. Lord, have mercy.

Lord Jesus, you give us the promise of everlasting life. Lord, have mercy.

I confess... *(all pray the confiteor)*

Our Father...

O my God, I thank you for loving me. I am sorry for all my sins, for not loving others and not loving you. Help me to live like Jesus and not sin again.

A familiar Act of Sorrow may be added.

Individual Confession and Absolution

We have the opportunity to celebrate the sacrament of penance. Approach any of the priests—be free to move around the church, to any of the priests. Allow people privacy by staying back a little.

Say something like, "I am sorry for all my sins and I want forgiveness." Mention serious sins as best you can. In other words, make a simple, brief, sincere confession of sin. You don't have to say any more. We have already expressed our sorrow.

The priest will pray the prayer of absolution. Return to your place and pray for one another.

The Rite of Penance *provides a primary source for suitable hymns, psalms, and prayers that may be used during this period of the service.*

Proclamation of Praise of God's Mercy

P   Let us proclaim God's mercy and give God thanks.

All   *Sing the Magnificat.*

Concluding Prayer of Thanksgiving

P   Let us pray.
God our Father, through the greatness of your love, we have access to your house. You have renewed the love we have wasted. We praise you. We thank you. We make our prayer through Christ our Lord. Amen.

Final Blessing

P   We have proclaimed and celebrated God's promise of forgiveness.
May the Father lavish love upon you.

R   Amen.

P   May Christ support you.

R   Amen.

P   May the Spirit fill you with joy.

R   Amen.

P   May almighty God, the Father and the Son ✠ and the Holy Spirit, bless you.

R   Amen.

P   Let us offer each other the sign of peace.

P   Go in that peace.

PARISH CELEBRATION III

Johnny Doherty, CSSR

The lighting in the church should be subdued with a spotlight on a cross or crucifix.

Opening Hymn
During the opening hymn, the book of the Scriptures is carried in in solemn procession, which should include all those who are to hear confessions; the book is solemnly enthroned near the crucifix and it is then incensed, after which the congregation is also incensed.

Introduction
P   We are gathered together to celebrate the wonder of our salva-
     tion. In the cross we have a powerful sign that our salvation has
     already taken place. In the sacrament of reconciliation we have
     the sign that our salvation is yet to be made complete in us. We
     are sinners, constantly in need of forgiveness.

   That is one of the great paradoxes of our faith: we are saved,
   and yet to be saved. The sacrament of reconciliation is part of
   the saving power that Christ has given his church.

   A good model for us to bring with us this evening is St. Dismas:
   a) He was a thief.
   b) He was very close to Jesus as our Savior died on the cross.
   c) He made one of the most amazing acts of faith, when he said,
   "Lord, remember me when you come into your kingdom." Jesus looked like anything but the Son of God at that moment.
   d) He teaches us that forgiveness is immediate and complete.
   "This day you will be with me in paradise," Jesus said.

Prayer

P Lord Jesus Christ,
we thank you for showing us how much you love us
by dying on a cross that we might live.
Strengthen us.
We pray that all of us here may have true repentance for our
sins. We ask forgiveness and healing in this sacrament, which
you gave your church.
We pray that each one of us may be filled with hope in your
love rather than despair because of the bonds of sin in our lives.
Take away all anxiety and fear from our hearts, and, as our sins
are forgiven again this evening, strengthen us to live in ways
that will make it easier for others to know your love and to live
your way.
Lord Jesus Christ, we pray to you as our Savior.
We know you as Son of God, who lives and reigns with the Father and the Holy Spirit, God for ever and ever.

R Amen.

Hymn

Gospel   Matthew 18:1–4

A reading from the holy Gospel according to Matthew.

At this time the disciples came to Jesus and said, "Who is the greatest in the kingdom of heaven?" So he called a little child to him and
set the child in front of them. Then he said, "I tell you solemnly, unless you change and become like little children you will never enter
the kingdom of heaven. And so, the one who makes himself as little
as this little child is the greatest in the kingdom of heaven."

The gospel of the Lord.

R Praise to you, Lord Jesus Christ.

Homily and Examination of Conscience

We may not want to be "the greatest" in heaven, but we do want to
get there. Jesus tells us that, to get there, we must become like little

children. Children have many qualities that are essential for living as God's children:

Trust: Look at a child in the arms of his or her parents; are we like that in our relationship with God?

Enthusiasm: Children look forward to almost everything; we take almost everything for granted.

Wonder: Look at a child at Christmas; the box is as important as the toy. We pass our days surrounded by beauty and we don't even notice it.

Forgiveness: A child can have a fight with someone one moment, and be friends the next. We hold grudges until the other person has been punished.

Innocence: Children ask a lot of questions and say a lot of outrageous things, but we can smile at them because we recognize the basic innocence of their minds and hearts. We have learned to be cautious, to manipulate, to be devious in so many ways. Often we have learned this as the way to survive.

When we examine our lives with the eyes of a child, we can easily find the ways in which we have to repent of our sins and to change so as to regain the freedom that God's grace brings us. We will now go back over those same characteristics and apply them more fully to ourselves.

Trust: We live in a world that is becoming increasingly materialistic. You have to look after number one. There is no room for trust in God's way of justice if you are going to get on in the world. That is so readily accepted today that it is destroying us.

— Do I do an honest day's work for an honest day's pay?

— Do I pay an honest wage to those who work for me? Or do I pay the minimum?

— Do I falsify tax returns and so put a burden on others?

— Do I take my place in fighting injustice in our society? Or do I leave it to others and so contribute to that injustice?

— Do I contribute to supporting the poor? Or do I see that what's mine is my own and has no reference to anyone else?

Innocence: When we say that someone has lost his or her innocence, we usually mean it in sexual terms. That is much too narrow an application because innocence involves our whole way of life. But our sexuality *is* central to life, and how we use our sexuality is significant in our response to God's desire for us.

— In reading books, papers, magazines, do I often look for sexual excitement?

— What do I look for in the TV programs I watch or the films I go to?

— How do I regard my own body? Do I abuse my gift of sexuality by promiscuous behavior?

— In my relationships with others do I follow God's way or is my standard simply: "If I feel like it, I do it"?

— Do I try to reverence the sexual dignity of others? Do I fail in this?

— Do I live by the standard of God's law that sexual intercourse is for marriage?

— In marriage, do I use my spouse sexually? Is there a lot of affection in how I treat her or him, or is intercourse simply an activity?

— Do I use sex in marriage as a bargaining power or as the free gift of myself?

Enthusiasm: Lift a child in the air and, when you put him or her down again, you'll almost always hear: "Do it again!" And if there's another child there, you'll hear: "Do it to me, too!"

— Is that the way I am with God and the things of God?

— Do I pray every day? Or does it depend on how I feel?

— Is my prayer enthusiastic or a bit of a drag?

— Do I go to Mass every Sunday and holy day?

— Do I take an active part in the Mass or do I leave that to others?

— Do I go to confession regularly?

— Am I open and honest when I go to confession?

— Am I involved in the parish in any active way?

— Am I willing to be involved in new ways to build up the life of the parish?

Sense of wonder: In adults, we see the loss of a sense of wonder about life. Drink and, in more recent times, drugs are such signs. These are entered into and abused most often out of boredom or a search for some "kick" out of life. They only lead to a further diminishing of the spirit.

— Do I drink to excess?

— How does my drinking affect my family and my friends?

— Do I encourage others to drink more than they want?

— Do I take drugs?

— Do I encourage others to take drugs?

— Do I spend a lot of money on my own pleasure and entertainment?

— Do I gamble a lot?

Forgiveness: Children don't hold grudges for very long. Adults can hold grudges for a lifetime.

— Is there anyone whom I find difficult to forgive?

— Who or what makes me angry in my family life, my life in church, my work life, my social life?

— Do I talk about and criticize particular people?

— Whom have I hurt by an angry word or action in my family, among my friends?

— Is there anyone in my family on whom I have given up and only meet when I have to?

P   We now publicly admit that each of us is a sinner. Let us say together:

All   I confess... *(all pray the confiteor)*

P   We also publicly acknowledge our sorrow by saying together an Act of Contrition...

P   Let us pray together in the words our Savior gave us:

All   Our Father...

Address before Confession

The priests will now go to various parts of the church. They will stand and you will stand with them. Ask him for either a blessing or for absolution. You may not need confession tonight—maybe because you were at this sacrament very recently or perhaps you may not be able to receive the sacrament at the moment because of something in your life. Mention that to the priest and he will pray with you and bless you in the name of the church.

If you want absolution, say that to the priest and then simply tell him the sins that you are conscious of.

The priest will place his hands on your shoulders to express the affection the church has for each one of us and also to make it easier to speak without being heard by others.

This is not a time for getting into discussion with the priest or seeking advice about a particular problem. Leave that, please, for another time.

When you have told your sins, the priest will give you absolution.

There is no need to say the Act of Contrition, as we have said it together already.

During this time we will pray and sing together. We will say the Rosary and sing a hymn between each decade. In this way, we can pray for one another right through this sacred time.

When everyone has had a chance to speak to a priest, we will all gather again for a final prayer and blessing.

Notes: *Have the Rosary arranged beforehand, with people deputed to lead it, special intentions for each decade that reflect the repentance and reconciliation of the parish, and with hymns between each decade.*

The priests should begin the process of individual confession by asking each other for a blessing or absolution just as we are asking our people to do.

Final Prayer and Blessing

After the individual confessions, all the priests should go to the front of the sanctuary, face the people and, as the leader prays, extend their hands over the congregation.

P   May God, the Father of mercies, through the intercession of our Blessed Lady, fill your hearts and your homes with peace. May God take away from you all anxiety and fear. May God heal all divisions that exist in your families and in our parish community, and may God bless all those you love. Together with them, may God bring you to everlasting life.

R   Amen.

P   May almighty God bless you, the Father, and the Son, ✠ and the Holy Spirit.

R   Amen.

Final Hymn

DURING A PARISH RETREAT I

Sean Moore, CSSR

The lighting in the church should be dimmed and it should be in semi-darkness as the participating priests enter in procession from the back. At the head of the procession, one priest carries a large crucifix with the figure facing toward himself. He places the crucifix on the altar, or at least in the sanctuary, in full view of all. The clergy file into seats facing the altar while the main celebrant goes directly to the ambo to begin the celebration.

Entrance Hymn
Sing "God of Mercy and Compassion," or another appropriate song.

Greeting
Dear friends, may the awareness of God's unconditional love and acceptance, together with the joy and peace of the Holy Spirit, be with you all.

Introduction
We have gathered for a public and communal celebration of the sacrament of reconciliation. All of us, of course, have so much and so often benefited from the "private" celebration of this sacrament. But Pope Paul VI has stated that "communal celebration shows more clearly the ecclesial nature of penance." Yes, our celebration this evening will help us realize that we are not just a group of individuals. We are a people, a parish, a family, a church. Together we are going to pray; together we are going to listen to God's word; together we are going to acknowledge our sinfulness, confessing quietly but publicly, and receiving God's loving forgiveness.

Let us now pray.
Lord, as we celebrate the sacrament of your loving kindness and forgiveness, we acknowledge that we have sinned personally and as a

community. Accept our desire to make amends and to reform our lives. Grant that the law of our community may be the law of Love. Make us one in mind and spirit. Our prayer we make, as always, through Christ Our Lord.

R   Amen.

LITURGY OF THE WORD

First Reading   Ephesians 4:1–3, 15–16, 23–32

This first reading has been used as an examination of conscience by Christians since the time of Christ. Let us listen to it now as our sisters and brothers have listened for almost 2000 years.

A reading from the letter of Paul to the Ephesians.

I implore you therefore to lead a life worthy of your vocation. Bear with one another charitably, in complete selflessness, gentleness and patience. Do all you can to preserve the unity of the Spirit by the peace that binds you together.

If we live by the truth and in love, we shall grow in all ways into Christ, who is the head by whom the whole body is fitted and joined together, every joint adding its own strength, for each separate part to work according to its function. So the body grows until it has built itself up, in love.

Your mind must be renewed by a spiritual revolution so that you can put on the new self that has been created in God's way, in the goodness and holiness of the truth.

So from now on, there must be no more lies: *You must speak the truth to one another*, since we are all parts of one another. *Even if you are angry, you must not sin*: never let the sun set on your anger or else you will give the devil a foothold. Anyone who was a thief must stop stealing; he should try to find some useful manual work instead, and be able to do some good by helping others that are in need. Guard against foul talk; let your words be for the improvement of others, as occasion offers, and do good to your listeners, otherwise you will only be grieving the Holy Spirit of God who has marked you with his seal for you to be set free when the day comes. Never have grudges against others, or lose your temper, or raise your voice to anybody, or call each other names, or allow any sort of spitefulness. Be friends with one another, and kind, forgiving each other as readily as God forgave you in Christ.

The word of the Lord.

R   Thanks be to God.

Responsorial Psalm   Psalm 62

R   In God alone there is rest for my soul.

1.   In God alone there is rest for my soul,
      from him comes my safety;
      with him alone for my rock, my safety,
      my fortress, I can never fall. R

2.   Rest in God, my safety, my glory,
      the rock of my strength.
      In God I find shelter; rely on him
      people, at all times;
      unburden your hearts to him,
      God is a shelter for us. R

Gospel   John 20:19–23

A reading from the holy Gospel according to John.

In the evening of that same day, the first day of the week, the doors were closed in the room where the disciples were, for fear of the Jews. Jesus came and stood among them. He said to them, "Peace be with you," and showed them his hands and his side. The disciples were filled with joy when they saw the Lord, and he said to them again, "Peace be with you.

"As the Father sent me,
so am I sending you."

After saying this he breathed on them and said:

"Receive the Holy Spirit.
For those whose sins you forgive,
they are forgiven;
for those whose sins you retain,
they are retained."

The gospel of the Lord.

R   Praise to you, Lord Jesus Christ.

Outline of Homily

1) We are dealing with a God whose name is love and whose attitude is that of understanding, acceptance, and forgiveness. Before us is the crucifix, the great symbol of our religion, the great symbol of God's love.

2) We need have no fear, then, to admit that we are sinners with weaknesses, infidelities, perversions, blindness.... And we can have hope. No one is a hopeless case; God does not regard our failures as final.

3) Indeed, admitting that we are sinners is the first step to a radical change in our life.

4) The communal nature of sin... because my sin affects and changes me, making me more selfish and less loving. It also affects those with whom I come into contact. It affects the community. Some sins are more obviously and dramatically anti-community—for example, murder, vandalism, adultery. Other sins may be secret but they are never private.

It seems that people in the early church were more aware of the social dimension of sin. They saw it as lowering the level of love in the community...failing to live by the values of the community.... They saw themselves as sinners owing it to the church to seek reconciliation with the community.

5) Forgiveness: "If you forgive... if you retain..." Tonight, as penitents, we are recognizing and acknowledging to the community that their love, acceptance, and forgiveness are enabling us in some way to experience the love, acceptance, and forgiveness of God. Power over sin resides and is exercised in the community. We can, and un-

fortunately do, withhold forgiveness at times. When we do that we are not contributing to the growth of love in the community and we are stunting our own growth as persons. Remember that in this sacrament we are celebrating not only God's forgiveness but also our own mutual forgiveness. Let us not bind the community in its sins.

So, as we celebrate God's love and forgiveness, let us also joyfully celebrate our love and forgiveness of one another.

Examination of Conscience
Already in this celebration, the Holy Spirit, through the words of the letter to the Ephesians, has helped us to examine our conscience. We now pause for a few moments to quietly reflect on how we have offended God and lowered the level of love in this parish community.

Confiteor
(recited together: pause for Act of Sorrow.)

Our Father
(Say together the prayer of God's family.)

Individual Confession and Absolution

Thanksgiving
Let us pray.
Father, most merciful and ever-loving God, we do well always and everywhere to give you thanks. We thank you for the grace and joy and healing that we have experienced in this celebration. Especially we thank you for the peace of heart that comes from knowing that our sins are forgiven and that we are always in the hands of our heavenly Father.

R   Amen.

Final Hymn of Thanksgiving
Sing "Now Thank We All Our God," or another appropriate song.

DURING A PARISH RETREAT II

Pat Collins and the Vincentian Mission Team

It is good to highlight the following three points during a parish mission.

1. Assure the people that, if they only look into the eyes of God's mercy, expecting only mercy, they will receive only mercy.

2. Invite the people to receive that liberating mercy by making—if they wish—a general confession of serious sins not previously confessed.

3. Encourage those who have experienced God's mercy to extend it to others, by living a merciful life.

Besides the missioners, parish clergy, and invited confessors, six members of the congregation are also needed, one to read the first Scripture reading, the others to read the five-part examination of conscience. Also needed are a five-branch candlestick (which is placed either on or in front of the altar), a box of matches, and a taper.

INTRODUCTORY RITES

Entrance Hymn

Sing "God of Mercy and Compassion," or another appropriate song.

Greeting

P   The grace of our Lord Jesus Christ, the love of God, and the fellowship of the Holy Spirit be with you all.

R   And also with you.

Introduction

Something on these lines would be appropriate:
In this service, Jesus says to each one of us, "Be merciful, just as your Father is merciful." He has shown us that there is no need to be afraid of God's justice. It is on hold, so to speak, until the day of judgment.

Meantime, we live in the age of boundless mercy. The good news can be summed up in these words: "If you only look into the eyes of God's mercy expecting only mercy, you will receive only mercy." While that mercy is available to all of us, we will only experience it to the extent that we are willing to try forgiving those people, living and dead, who have hurt, injured, or offended us in any way.

Opening Prayer
Lord, our hearts are restless. Whatever the cost, we desire at this time a fuller conversion of mind and heart. Let our sins be forgiven, haunting memories forgotten, broken relationships healed, compulsive patterns of action ended, unfounded fears resolved, and distorted thinking made right, so that we may enjoy the peace and freedom of God's children. We ask this through Jesus Christ our Lord.

R   Amen.

LITURGY OF THE WORD

First Reading

Either:

Sirach 28:2–7 *especially if the priest celebrant intends giving his own homily.*

Forgive your neighbor the hurt he does you,
and when you pray, your sins will be forgiven.
If a man nurses anger against another,
can he then demand compassion from the Lord?
Showing no pity for a man like himself,
can he then plead for his own sins?
Mere creature of flesh, he cherishes resentment;
who will forgive him his sins?
Remember the last things, and stop hating.

or:

Micah 7:18–19 *if the priest celebrant intends recounting the parable below.*

What god can compare with you: taking fault away,
pardoning crime,

not cherishing anger for ever
but delighting in showing mercy?
Once more have pity on us,
tread down our faults,
to the bottom of the sea
throw all our sins.

Hymn

"The Lord Is My Shepherd," or any version of Psalm 23 known by those assembled.

Gospel   Luke 6:36–38

A reading from the holy Gospel according to Luke.

Be compassionate as your Father is compassionate. Do not judge, and you will not be judged yourselves; do not condemn, and you will not be condemned yourselves; grant pardon, and you will be pardoned. Give, and there will be gifts for you: a full measure, pressed down, shaken together, and running over, will be poured into your lap; because the amount you measure out is the amount you will be given back.

The gospel of the Lord.

R   Praise to you, Lord Jesus Christ.

Homily

Here are two suggestions:
a) The priest may give a short talk of about five to ten minutes in length which could stress the following points:

1) The boundless mercy and love of God.
2) That in the light of that mercy it is safe to admit one's sins to oneself, to God, and to another human being who in this instance is a priest who represents the forgiving Christ and the Christian community in the sacrament of reconciliation. As James said, "So confess your sins to one another, and pray for one another, and this will cure you" (James 5:16).

3) To ask the Lord who enlightens every heart to enlighten those in the congregation, to recognize the things that quench the Spirit of God within them, such as resentments, and to recognize their root causes, such as pride and selfishness.

4) To give clear, practical advice about the way in which to make confession, such as by suggesting what might be mentioned, and possibly a penance to be performed, such as where it is necessary to be reconciled with neighbors, relatives, or estranged friends.

b) The priest could recount this parable in his own words:

A sinner was walking dejectedly by a lakeside. Eventually he met a boatman who, unbeknownst to him, was the Lord. The boatman said, "I'm going for a row across the lake, would you like to come?" Having nothing better to do, the sinner said a little hesitantly, "Yes, I'd like to if it is O.K. with you." With that, the two men got into the boat.

The sinner sat in the front. As a result, he was facing the Lord, who had chosen to sit in the middle. The Lord picked up the oars and off they went, gently gliding across the calm water. The sinner felt at ease with the boatman; he was the kind of person you could talk to—a good listener, compassionate and understanding. At first he engaged in small talk. But then, encouraged by the boatman's warm personality, he began to talk about himself.

At first he didn't reveal anything of any importance. But, as he sensed the sympathetic responses of his mysterious companion, the sinner began to reveal more of the truth about his life. All the while, he kept nervously glancing at the boatman to see if there was any hint of aversion, shock, or repulsion in his eyes. He was relieved to see that they were constant and unperturbed, devoid of any hint of criticism or condemnation. However, the sinner noticed that whenever he revealed some new failing or weakness, the boatman seemed to put each of them into a sack at his feet.

By now the sinner was opening up as never before. Although there was a fear of rejection in his heart, he was energized by an even stronger desire to reveal the whole truth about himself. It gave him the courage to open up the doors of his memory to reveal the secret skeletons that had been hidden there for quite some time. As he spoke, he couldn't even look the oarsman in the eye. Nevertheless, he told him about all the most shameful incidents in his life.

When he got to the end, he glanced up at the boatman. He felt an immense sense of relief when he saw that he was as understanding as ever. For the last time, the boatman opened the sack and popped in the guilty secrets he had just heard.

By now the boat had reached the middle of the lake. The boatman put up the oars. Then he tied the top of the sack and attached it to a heavy stone that lay at the back of the boat. He invited the sinner to look over the side as he threw the sack into the lake. The two men watched as it sank ever deeper through the clear, fresh waters, until it disappeared out of sight. The boatman gave his hands a couple of satisfied rubs and said, "Well, that's the end of that lot."

Then he took up the oars again. He had no sooner done so, when he said, "Oh, I have forgotten something." He put down the oars and reached behind him to the back of the boat. This time he produced a small float with a flag on it. This he set bobbing on the water, in the exact place where he had thrown in the sack. On it were inscribed the words,"No fishing here!" Having done so, he lifted up the oars and began the journey back to the shore.

The two men chatted all the way. In next to no time they were back at their starting point. They shook hands in an animated fashion and parted. The sinner went off whistling a happy tune while the boatman returned to his cottage, which was nearby.

Early the next morning, the boatman was roused by the sound of urgent knocking. He went to the door and there was the sinner crestfallen and dejected. "Oh, it is you," the boatman exclaimed, "What has happened to upset you so much?" "I have fallen again," replied the sinner in a whisper. "Again," responded the Lord, "but when was the last time?"

There are two morals in this story. First, an honest confession of our weaknesses and failings is a liberating experience. They are swallowed up in the bottomless waters of God's mercy. You should never fish them up again with their attendant feelings of guilt. As Hebrews 8:12 assures us, they are forgiven and forgotten forever. There will be no record of them on judgment day. Second, if perchance you fail again, there is no need to be afraid; the Lord will have no memory of your previous offenses and will forgive you again and again with great compassion and gentleness. All that the Lord asks in return is that we forgive one another as God has forgiven us and show mercy to others, especially the poor and disadvantaged.

Examination of Conscience

At this point most of the lights in the church are dimmed or turned off alto-gether. However, there is need for adequate lighting at the lectern where the readers from the congregation will read their respective sections of the ex-amination of conscience. Ideally, each one should have a copy. Having read his or her section, each person lights one of the five candles, the first with a match, the others with a taper, which is ignited from the last candle lit.

1) My relationship with God.
> Lord I am sorry.
> I sometimes thought that you sent suffering and death to my family...
> I often felt that you ignored my prayers and tears and that you couldn't be bothered with me...
> I was angry with you... I envied other people who didn't seem to suffer at all...

> I am sorry Lord...truly sorry.

> There were times when I didn't respect your holy name...
> There were times when I didn't worship you in my heart or with your people in the Eucharist...

> I am sorry Lord...truly sorry.

2) My relationship with my family, other people, and myself.
> I ask to be forgiven because I hurt my family, my parents, those who taught me, and my children.

At this point in my life, I am willing to let go of the resentful spirit of ingratitude that prevented me saying either the words, "thank you" or "I love you."
There is that concealed sin that makes me feel ashamed and guilty.
There were times in the past when I didn't live with dignity... when I lacked self-control...
There were times when I failed to respect those around me... when I was exploitive, manipulative, dishonest, and unjust...
For those times when I sinned against decency, when I sinned against purity or charity...

I am sorry Lord...truly sorry.

3) I forgive members of my family.

In my heart, I now ask the Lord for the grace to want to forgive my father and mother for the times they hurt me, for the times they quarreled...drank too much...and failed to love me in the way I needed to be loved...
I forgive them for the times they hurt each other and made me feel anxious and insecure...
I forgive them for their many put-downs and lack of affirmation and praise...
I truly forgive my brother or sister for the times that they hurt me because of what they said or did to me...
I truly forgive my partner and my children for any heartache they have caused me...for any painful lack of love on their part...
I also forgive those who interfered and brought unhappiness...

4) I forgive my neighbors and co-workers.

Lord, forgive me for the times I have hurt other people, either by ignoring their needs and their pain or by being critical and judgmental in my attitudes and conversation.
Jesus, I ask for the grace to forgive those outside my home with whom I share my life.

Help me to forgive those who make life difficult for me, those who disturb my peace and cause me sleepless nights...those who make it hard for me to face another day...

Help me to forgive those who have misjudged me…those who have betrayed my trust…those who have taken advantage of me…or those who have cheated or injured or abused me in any way…

5) Help me to forgive the person who has hurt me the most.

Jesus, enable me to forgive the person who failed to stand by me when times were hard…

Give me the grace to forgive the person I find it hardest to forgive, the person who hurt and injured me the most…

You promise us all we need…now I ask for the grace to forgive, to overcome bitterness and resentment and to be at peace…

Lord Jesus, it is almost impossible to forgive, to turn the other cheek, to give to those who have already hurt me in some way…but you forgive me and you ask me to be forgiving in the same way…I can't do so without your help, so now I pray for the healing power of your forgiveness in this sacrament.

Lord, make me an instrument of your peace.
Where there is hatred, let me sow love,
Where there is injury, pardon,
Where there is darkness, light,
and where there is sadness, joy.
For it is in giving that we receive,
It is in pardoning that we are pardoned,
And it is in dying that we are born to eternal life. Amen.

LITURGY OF RECONCILIATION

Confession

The presiding priest tells the people where the available confessors will be located and gives them some pointers as to how to make their confession, e.g. "Why not mention the sin that has been bothering you the most? There is no need to dot all your i's and cross all your t's. The Lord knows every- thing that is in your heart, but if you wish to make a general confession, feel free to do so now or later in the mission. But, because of the numbers here at the moment, we won't have time to discuss personal problems or to offer counseling. If you need to have a chat, make an appointment to see one of the priests at a convenient time."

Communal Act of Contrition and Lord's Prayer

Individual Confessions

Three small altar lights may be placed near each confessor. Explain to the people that they symbolize how the mercy of God can fill our past, present, and future lives through the sacrament.

The choir/music group quietly sings appropriate hymns, such as "Amazing Grace" or "Christ Be Beside Me," during the confessions.

CONCLUDING RITE

Final Exhortation

Thanks to visiting priests, readers, choir/music group and the people for coming. They are encouraged to bury the hatchet and to be reconciled as soon as possible with people who need their forgiveness.

Concluding Prayer

Father in heaven,
thank you for forgiving us our sins.

From this time forward give us the power with all your holy people to know the length and the breadth, the height and the depth of the love of Jesus, which surpasses understanding, so that, experiencing that love, we may extend it to others, especially those who need our forgiveness. We ask this through the same Christ our Lord.

R   Amen.

Blessing

Dismissal

Final Hymn

Sing a song celebrating God's forgiveness and our mission to bring the good news to the poor.

SMALL GROUP I

Pierce Murphy

Theme: Pure Religion

Opening Hymn
"Grant to Us, O Lord, a Heart Renewed" or the psalm with refrain.

Introduction

We have been together for some time now, struggling to increase our faith, to broaden our hope, and deepen our love of God and of our neighbor. We come to look at our lives in relation to God our Father, to see our strengths and our weaknesses; to confess to our loving and forgiving God and to be joyfully reconciled with God and with each other. Then we can live as true sons and daughters of our God.

We have chosen the theme of "Pure Religion" or, to put it another way, "What does God ask of me, of us?" Our reflection comes from the prophet Micah. He has been reminding the people of the great wonders Yahweh, their God, has done for them. They want to respond. They want to respond with sacrifices and burnt offerings. Then Micah gives Yahweh's answer as follows:

Reader:

> This is what Yahweh asks of you:
> only this, to act justly,
> to love tenderly
> and to walk humbly with your God. (Micah 6:8)

> The word of the Lord.

R   Thanks be to God.

The reader or celebrant leads the reflection. The group could be invited to share on some or all of the points:

> Does this passage surprise you?
> Does it remind you of anything Jesus said? (Matthew 25:40:
> "...did it to me.")

Let us take each sentence:

To act justly

Reflection: We can see people doing their everyday jobs with care, concern, and honesty. They know that they are lucky to have jobs and are concerned for others. Many a mother, or indeed a father now, spends time quietly rearing children to take their place in society and have good Christian values. An eagerness to work with a sense of fair play and justice is just one of the values they pass on. They are generous to people in need, both those near at home and those in the third world countries. Many young people are really incensed at the exploitation, poverty, and destruction often caused by greed for possessions or for power. They actively work to relieve this. Sometimes we see people who seem to have a double standard of justice when they are dealing with the government or big business. Other times people, by their unfair comments or gossip, can ruin another person or company.

Points to ponder:

Am I lazy or energetic?
Do I think of others or am I selfish?
How concerned am I for people who are starving?
Are my comments about others fair and just?
What is my attitude in dealing with government, taxes, etc.?
How do I treat my employer and his or her property and time?

Sharing, if appropriate

Period of silence (music)

Prayer

P   God our Father, be with us as we struggle to act justly in our lives. Help us to realize that we have received many blessings. Help us to have a spirit of openness and generosity in our lives so that we can show your love to others. This we ask through Christ our Lord.

R   Amen.

Love Tenderly

Reflection: The values that produce tender love between people don't come from television or novels, they come from deep within us. They reflect how God loved us first and has made us for God's love. Whether we are married or single, these values enable us to be lifegiving for others. Often these values are not there in some of our relationships and there is often a gruff selfishness that sees others as objects, objects to be used or to give pleasure.

We can contrast this with the homely picture of a father or mother picking up the child for the nth time at night, or the husband and wife settling down to relax and talk together when the children are in bed, or fathers and mothers working hard for their families, whether out in business or in the home, or the young couple in love, tenderly yet respectfully preparing for their marriage, or the teenage family who respectfully and lovingly work to make their home happy.

Points to ponder:
> How can I love my partner more tenderly?
> How can I spend more time with him or her?
> Do I see people as people to be loved or used?
> How can I help people to grow in love rather than stunt their growth?
> What people do I exclude from my love?
> Am I faithful to my partner, to my friends?
> Do I pass on God's pattern for loving or the media's?

Sharing, if appropriate

Period of silence (music)

Prayer

P   God our Father, it is your love of us that inspires our love of others. Help our love to grow more tender so that your love in us will reach perfection. This we ask through Christ our Lord.

R   Amen.

Walk humbly with God

Reflection: Jesus told the story of the Pharisee and the tax collector. The tax collector clearly saw his position before God and would only stand at the door asking for forgiveness. He knew his strengths and weaknesses before God. We know that we are made in the image and likeness of God, and that gives us a great dignity and worth. We also know that without God's help we have little or no chance of living up to that dignity. If we leave God out of our lives, we are putting ourselves at the center of our world and very often we leave ourselves there in our frustration with ourselves. With God, all things are possible. So in our daily prayer, we can praise God for God's great love of us, ask God's help for the future, and beg God's pardon for the past.

Points to ponder:
> Where does God come into my life?
> How can I give more time to prayer?
> Do I praise and thank God, especially at Mass?
> Do I thank God for my successes or just blame God for my failures?
> How do I respect God and God's name?
> Do I respect others who walk with God, too?

Sharing, if appropriate

Period of silence (music)

Responsorial Psalm   Psalm 51

R   Have mercy on me, O God, in your goodness,
     in your great tenderness wipe away my faults.

1.   God, create a clean heart in me,
     put into me a new and constant spirit,
     do not banish me from your presence
     do not deprive me of your holy spirit. R

2.   Save me from death, God my savior,
     and my tongue will proclaim your righteousness;
     Lord, open my lips,
     and my mouth will speak out your praise. R

3.   Sacrifice gives you no pleasure,
     were I to offer holocaust, you would not have it.
     My sacrifice is this broken spirit,
     you will not scorn this crushed and broken heart. R

Reading

Micah again or James 1:19–27 or Matthew 25:31–36

Act of Sorrow

For the injustices I have caused to others, directly or indirectly.
Lord, have mercy. R
For the lack of love in my life, especially for those close to me.
Christ, have mercy. R
For the times I have made myself the center of my life.
Lord, have mercy. R

All   I confess ... *(all pray the confiteor)*

P   Let us pray together in the words our Savior gave us:

All   Our Father ...

If there is to be sacramental confession, the individual confessions now take place. Alternatively, the service may simply be concluded with a prayer of forgiveness like:

May almighty God have mercy on us, forgive us our sins, and bring us to life everlasting. Amen. (*From the Penitential Rite of Mass*)

P   Let us give each other a sign of peace—a sign of the surety of
     God's forgiveness and an offer of support for the future.

Psalm of Thanks

e.g Psalm 136 v 1, 2, 3, 4, 6, 23, 24, 25, 26.
Response: God's love is everlasting.

Priest leads prayer together:

P   God, Father of the humble walkers,
     be with us in each new step,
     guide our faltering feet,
     warm our cool hearts,
     sustain our just dealings
     as we struggle to make your world
     a better place to live in.
     This we ask through Christ our Lord.

R   Amen.

P   Go in peace to walk with God.

R   Amen.

Hymn

"Hymn of Micah," or "Christ Be With Me," or another appropriate song.

SMALL GROUP II

New Year's Eve Family Celebration

I used this simple adaptation of Young People II (James Doherty) for a very successful family celebration at midnight on New Year's Eve.—Oliver Crilly

I: PENITENTIAL RITE

Taizé music
Crucifix in center. Candle lighted before it. Two groups of children enter from opposite sides, in dark clothes, and glare at each other. Hold position. Then slowly they all turn to face the crucifix. They turn slowly to look at each other again, then take off their jackets or coats to reveal white shirts or tops or brightly colored dresses. They step toward each other, take each other's hands, and make peace. Then they all simply kneel before the crucifix. They stay kneeling for the reading.

Gospel   Matthew 5:23–24

A reading from the holy Gospel according to Matthew.

If you are bringing your offering to the altar and there remember that your brother has something against you, leave your offering there before the altar, go and be reconciled with your brother first, and then come back and present your offering.
The gospel of the Lord.

R   Praise to you, Lord Jesus Christ.

Intercessions

For the times we have allowed our feelings to rule our lives and make us hurtful to those around us, Lord, have mercy. R
For the times we have closed our fists and our hearts to others, Lord, have mercy. R
For the times we have refused to walk with our brothers and sisters, Lord, have mercy. R

P   Let us pray together in the words Jesus gave us:

All   Our Father…

Taizé music
Each person present goes forward in his or her turn, kneels for quite a long time in front of the crucifix, asking God's forgiveness and offering his or her life to God, to try to do God's will in the New Year. Then each returns quietly to his or her place. All say together the Act of Sorrow.

II: HYMNS AND READINGS

A liturgy of the word follows, to the following outline:

Hymn

First Reading

Psalm

Second Reading

Alleluia verse

Gospel

Short shared reflection

Taizé music
Each person receives a picture of Christ, the ruler of all the world. A candle is lighted and brought in procession to the table where everyone will have some food and drink, the first shared meal of the New Year.

DURING A SCHOOL RETREAT I

John McKenna

Step 1

Introduction

Imagine for a moment that you are locked away in a cold and damp basement by people who just grabbed you on the street and never gave a reason. Imagine also that the people who did this blindfolded you, chained you to a wall, and deprived you of all communication with others. Left alone in that silent, dark world you would have nothing but your thoughts to keep you sane.

Terrible as it may seem, something like that happened to totally innocent men in Beirut during the civil war there. These men became known simply as the "hostages."

All these men were held unjustly. They did nothing to deserve their fate. They were beaten, tortured, and blindfolded for most of their captivity. It would seem that now they are at least entitled to complain and feel sorry for themselves.

The amazing thing about all the hostages is that not one of them has ever expressed a single word of revenge or hatred. For example, one of the released hostages, Brian Keenan, at a press conference in Dublin, said, "I feel no hatred."

In our lives we too experience unjust treatment. This can happen in many ways.

> Sometimes we are wrongly blamed.
> Sometimes we hear rumors and we feel hurt.
> It can happen that our friends let us down.
> We may even experience violence against us.

In all these situations, we feel anger and resentment rising up inside us. We feel entitled to get revenge. Yet we have the ability, with God's grace, to rise above these feelings and say "I'm sorry" or "I forgive you."

In this penitential service, we will reflect on the times we have failed to show love. We will listen to the word of God, and make promises for the future.

We think about how we show love for ourselves, and we remember that a person who does this will:

> Treat the body with respect.
> Avoid over-indulgence in such things as alcohol and food.
> Use sexuality properly and treat it as a gift from God.
> Exercise and lead a healthy lifestyle.

Now we call to mind all the times we have failed to show love for ourselves and abused the gift of life God has given us.

> For the times when I lost confidence in myself.
> Forgive me, Lord.
> For the times when I lost hope in everything and felt
> bitter and resentful to others.
> Forgive me, Lord.
> For the times when I sulked and felt sorry for myself.
> Forgive me, Lord.

Now that we have thought about and prayed for forgiveness, we sum up all our thoughts and feelings in this short prayer:

God of power and mercy,
we have expressed our sorrow
for the times we have failed to show love.
Come into our lives now
with the love you showed to your friends
and help us to love others the way you did.

R   Amen.

The following scriptural references may be used to find words in the Bible that pertain to forgiveness, reconciliation, and peace and may be used as "one-liners" where appropriate.

Psalm 41:5: Cure me, for I have sinned against you.

103:12: He takes our sins farther away than the east is from the west.

Isaiah 1:18: Your sins... shall be as white as snow.

2:4: ...swords into plowshares...

11:6: ...calf and lion cub feed together...

58:1–11: ... your light will rise in the darkness...

Hosea 11:3: I took them in my arms.

Matthew 3:1–12: Repent for the kingdom of heaven is close at hand.

5:7: Happy the merciful, they shall have mercy shown them.

5:9: Happy the peacemakers.

5:23–25 Go and be reconciled.

5:39: If anyone hits you on the right cheek...

6:12: Forgive us our debts.

18:15–18: If your brother does something wrong...

18:21–22: Not seven, I tell you, but seventy-seven times...

18:35: Unless you each forgive your brother...

Mark 2: 1–12: Who can forgive sins but God?

11:25: Forgive whatever you have against anybody.

Luke 5:8: Leave me, Lord; I am a sinful man.

7:36–50: ...her sins, her many sins, must have been forgiven her.

11:3–4: Forgive us our sins...

15:11–32: Father, I have sinned against heaven and against you.

17:1–4: If your brother does something wrong, reprove him and, if he is sorry, forgive him.

18:9–14: God, be merciful to me, a sinner.

23:34: Father, forgive them.

John 8:1–11: ...go away and don't sin any more.

Step 2

Examination of Conscience

We pause for a few moments and examine our lives to see if there are any ways in which we are failing to show love. We think about the ways we show love for God, for others, and for ourselves.

A person who shows love for God will:

Make God the most important person in life.

Value everything as a gift from God.
Realize that he or she owes life itself to God.
Praise and worship God.

Think for a moment about the quality of your own love for God. Perhaps God wants to draw your attention to something in your relationship with God.

Lord, for the times I ignored you, even though I felt your presence in different ways, Lord, have mercy.

Lord, sometimes I put other people and places and things before you. For all the times I failed to give you your proper place in my life, Lord, have mercy.

A person who shows love for others will:
Be willing to love others as brothers and sisters in the human family of God.
Respect the good name of other people.
Speak well of others.
Help out when the need arises.

There are many times, however, when we fail to live up to these ideals of love. So at this moment we pause and call to mind what we need to do to be more loving toward others:

For the times I refused to speak to the people who hurt me, I'm sorry, Lord.

For the times I tried to get revenge and tried to hurt others by speaking poorly of them, I'm sorry, Lord.

Step 3

Readings

So far in our penitential service we have expressed our sorrow for failing to show love to God, to others, and to ourselves. Now we spend time listening to God's word. We believe that God speaks to us through the Scriptures, and somewhere in the readings you may find encouragement that will help you to become a more loving person.

The celebrant may choose from any of the following:

Luke 15:1–7   (The Lost Sheep)
Luke 15:8–10   (The Lost Coin)
Luke 15:11–20   (The Parable of the Father and Son)
John 13:33–39   (The New Commandment to Love)
1 John 4:11–16   (God is love)
1 Corinthians 13   (St. Paul's description of love)

The prayer of St. Francis is very appropriate in the context of these readings:

Lord make me an instrument of your peace.
Where there is hatred, let me sow love.
Where there is doubt, faith.
Where there is despair, hope.
Where there is darkness, light.
Where there is sadness, joy.

Grant that I may not so much seek
to be consoled as to console,
to be understood as to understand,
to be loved as to love.

For it is in giving that we receive;
it is in pardoning that we are pardoned,
and it is in dying that we are born to eternal life.

Step 4

Looking to the Future
In this prayer service we have reflected on life and asked forgiveness for the times when we have failed to show love. God has spoken to us in the readings and we have learned something of how God wants to touch our lives with love. Now we look to the future.

We have learned how hard it is to forgive:

Is there someone in my life at the present time who is waiting for me to show forgiveness? Am I ready to make an approach to that person and show in some way that I am willing to forgive?

We know how hard it is to accept forgiveness:
Is there someone in my life who has tried to offer forgiveness and I refuse to accept because I feel weak or foolish or proud? Am I ready now to make an approach to that person and accept forgiveness?

We know how many times we could have been peacemakers in our class, our family, and our neighborhood.
Is there some situation in class or family or neighborhood where I am ready now to show a more positive attitude—to indicate to others that I am willing to take a lead and bring a little happiness into their lives?

In this part of our service, God has called us to face the future with confidence in God's love. Now, as we finish our penitential service, we are more aware of what the future holds for us and perhaps in some way we may bring God's love into the lives of others. Perhaps God wants to reach other people through you and me. In that spirit, we finish our service with the words:

Go in peace to love and serve the Lord.

DURING A SCHOOL RETREAT II

Margaret McEntee

The room:
Ideally this service should take place in the school oratory or religion room.
The room should be darkened. Only candles and a reading lamp provide
light. Symbols of life and death, such as colorful plants and some dead tree-
bark might provide a focal point. These could be referred to at the introduc-
tion to the service.

Opening Song
I found "Whenever God Shines His Light on Me," by Cliff Richards, appro-
priate. I played it on tape and made sure that each student had a copy of the
words.

Introduction
by teacher or school chaplain

I would like to welcome everybody to today's penance service. We
are here to reflect on our lives, to look at ourselves as we really are,
calmly and with honesty before God. God is here with us. God's love
and forgiveness is available to us. All we have to do is ask.

Opening Prayer
Let us pray.
God our Father, you are full of forgiveness.
We come before you today as we are,
trying to lead a good life, but sometimes failing.
May we go from this place healed
and made whole by your forgiving hand.
This we ask through Christ our Lord.

R   Amen.

First Reading   Romans 12:14–20

A reading from the letter of Paul to the Romans.

Bless those who persecute you: never curse them, bless them. Rejoice with those who rejoice and be sad with those in sorrow. Treat everyone with equal kindness; never be condescending but make real friends with the poor. Do not allow yourself to become self-satisfied. Never repay evil with evil but let everyone see that you are interested only in the highest ideals. Do all you can to live at peace with everyone. Never try to get revenge; leave that, my friends, to God's anger. As scripture says: *Vengeance is mine—I will pay them back,* the Lord promises. But there is more: *If your enemy is hungry, you should give him food, and if he is thirsty, let him drink. Thus you heap red-hot coals on his head.* Resist evil and conquer it with good.

The word of the Lord.

R   Thanks be to God.

Response in Song
Sing "Make Me a Channel of Your Peace," or another appropriate song.

Examination of Conscience
This examination of conscience could be read by two or three students. When finished, invite the students to read it again privately and reflect for some minutes. Soft music could be played during this exercise.

In my relationships with others, do I show kindness and consideration, or do I always put myself and my needs first?

Do I respect the right of others to a good reputation, or am I eager for the first bit of hot gossip in order to spread rumor and half-truth?

Do I make an effort to befriend and talk to those who are on the fringes of groups, or do I bask in the security of knowing that I have friends and make no effort?

In relation to school work, do I make an honest effort, or do I try anything to get out of work...daydreaming, wasting time, skipping homework?

In my after-school job, do I do an honest day's work for an honest day's pay?

Am I honest in my dealings with other people's money, property, books, etc.?

In my family, do I make an effort to pull my weight by helping with chores, defusing tension rather than creating it?

Do I have an open and honest relationship with my parents: free of deceit and lies?

Do I make an effort to develop my relationship with God by thinking about my faith and where I'm going in my life?

Do I pray with any consistency or only when I'm in trouble?

In my sexual relationships, am I careful to respect myself and the other person?

Do I respect my body as God-given and make an effort not to pollute it by over-indulgence in food, drink, cigarettes, etc.?

Individual Confession

If the school chaplain or other priest is available, the students may wish to avail themselves of the sacrament of penance. The priest sits in a quiet corner of the room and the students approach him, mention some sin, and express their sorrow for all their sins. This should be followed by a short Act of Contrition and absolution. Make sure that the students have a copy of a simple act of contrition, as a lack of this can cause confusion.

During this time of confession the opening song could be played again and the students asked to reflect on the words.

If no priest is present, the Act of Sorrow should be said together, followed by a short prayer for forgiveness said by the leader.

Lord, have mercy (*sung*)

Reading   Psalm 67

May God show kindness and bless us,
and make his face smile on us!

For then the earth will acknowledge your ways
and all the nations will know of your power to save.

Let the nations praise you, O God,
let all the nations praise you!

Let the nations shout and sing for joy,
since you dispense true justice to the world;
on earth you rule the nations.

Let the nations praise you, God,
Let all the nations praise you!

The word of the Lord.

R   Thanks be to God.

Prayer

Lord, we thank you for your forgiveness and love. Help us to go from here with forgiveness in our hearts for ourselves and others, confident that you will be with us in our struggle to do good and avoid evil.

This we ask through Christ our Lord.

R   Amen.

Blessing

May the Lord bless us, look kindly on us, and give us peace.

R   Amen.

Final Song

Sing "Awake from Your Slumber," or another appropriate song.

YOUNG PEOPLE I

Joe McDermott

Opening Hymn
Sing "Father Mercy" (Saint Louis Jesuits), or another appropriate song.

P   In the Name of the Father, and of the Son, and of the Holy Spirit.

R   Amen.

P   The peace of the Lord be with you always.

R   And also with you.

P   In our lives, we experience, on the one hand, goodness, peace, joy, and love, and, on the other, evil, pain, suffering, and hatred. These are caused by people. Within each of us is the potential for good and for evil. It is difficult, even painful, to confront ourselves with the reality of our own lives, and to take responsibility for the pain and suffering we have caused to others. God calls us to grow. We want to change, and we know we can. Through Jesus, we are assured of God's love and forgiveness.

The pain and suffering that Jean Vanier noticed in his book, *Be Not Afraid*, is the same pain and suffering that touches all our lives and the lives of those around us. Let us reflect on the following passage:

If I truly love
if I feel concerned
my life must change

My life must change
the life I have built for myself
must be destroyed

must be completely changed

the time I get up and go to bed
the friends I like to talk with
> *go out with*
> *eat with in smart restaurants*
the books I read
the money I have to spend

If I enter the world of touch
> *the world of tender compassion*
> *the world of the prisoner, the handicapped, the hungry,*
my whole way of life is in danger of falling apart.
I am in danger of entering a world of insecurity.

And yet we need security
those landmarks
which let us know where we are
and perhaps let us know ourselves a little

If I become truly open
> *open to the suffering of others*
my life will change
I will change
It's too much
I'm afraid.

So better cross the street
> *not stop by the half-dead man*
> *not look at him*
> *not visit the prisons, the handicapped, the sick.*

Or if I do stop
invent reasons
> *not to become involved*
> *not to give myself*
> *not to touch them*
> *not to become committed.*

Exciting theories!

Society had better change!
Abolish poverty!
I'll start a revolution
I'll solve everything
There won't be any more poor people!

Or I'll go back to my books
        to my humane or revolutionary talk
I'll escape to drugs, to television, to eroticism
        or throw myself into hyperactivity
        work to make money
        not knowing how to spend it
        on increasingly
                useless
                suicidal luxuries
        which kill
        by comfort
I'll escape the poor, the suffering, the forsaken
I'll flee the world of compassion.

Gospel   Luke 15:11–32

A reading from the holy Gospel according to Luke.

Jesus also said, "A man had two sons. The younger said to his father, 'Father, let me have the share of the estate that would come to me.' So the father divided the property between them. A few days later the younger son got together everything he had and left for a distant country where he squandered his money on a life of debauchery.

"When he had spent it all, that country experienced a severe famine, and now he began to feel the pinch, so he hired himself out to one of the local inhabitants who put him on his farm to feed the pigs. And he would willingly have filled his belly with the husks the pigs were eating but no one offered him anything. Then he came to his senses and said, 'How many of my father's paid servants have more food than they want, and here I am dying of hunger! I will leave this place and go to my father and say: Father, I have sinned against heaven and against you; I no longer deserve to be called your son; treat me as one of your paid servants.' So he left the place and went back to his father.

"While he was still a long way off, his father saw him and was moved with pity. He ran to the boy, clasped him in his arms and kissed him tenderly. Then his son said, 'Father, I have sinned against heaven and against you. I no longer deserve to be called your son.' But the father said to his servants, 'Quick! Bring out the best robe and put it on him; put a ring on his finger and sandals on his feet. Bring the calf we have been fattening, and kill it; we are going to have a feast, a celebration, because this son of mine was dead and has come back to life; he was lost and is found.' And they began to celebrate.

"Now the elder son was out in the fields, and on his way back, as he drew near the house, he could hear music and dancing. Calling one of the servants he asked what it was all about. 'Your brother has come,' replied the servant, 'and your father has killed the calf we had fattened because he has got him back safe and sound.' He was angry then and refused to go in, and his father came out to plead with him; but he answered his father, 'Look, all these years I have slaved for you and never once disobeyed your orders, yet you never offered me so much as a kid for me to celebrate with my friends. But, for this son of yours, when he comes back after swallowing up your property— he and his women—you kill the calf we had been fattening.'

"The father said, 'My son, you are with me always and all I have is yours. But it was only right we should celebrate and rejoice, because your brother here was dead and has come to life; he was lost and is found.'"

The gospel of the Lord.

R   Praise to you, Lord Jesus Christ.

Suggestions for Homily
The homilist might like to point out the stages of the reconciliation process between the prodigal son and his father. The son first came to an awareness of what he had done. He decided to do something about it. Having made his decision to change, he returned to the fa-

ther. In the father he encountered not the blame he had expected, but complete forgiveness. He was welcomed back as a son, not as a hired servant as he had expected.

Examination of Conscience

P   Let us reflect on our lives, so that we, too, may come to an awareness of our sinfulness. Let us think of the way we live with, and relate to, others.

Have I been responsible for divisions, anguish, rejection in my family? *(pause)*

In my relationships with others, have I used people selfishly—friends, work associates, etc.? *(pause)*

Have I been honest in my relationships and in my responsibilities? *(pause)*

Have I offered my time, talents, and resources to help those most in need—the poor, the marginalized, the lonely, the suffering? *(pause)*

Have I taken responsibility for my own growth in faith? *(pause)*

Do I make time for God through reflection and prayer? *(pause)*

Do I allow my belief in God and God's message to challenge the attitudes and values that rule my life? *(pause)*

Is my belief in God a mere habit or convention? *(pause)*

Have I taken responsibility for building the kingdom of God in our world—or have I opted for a kingdom based on the attitudes and values of today's world? *(pause)*

Act of Repentance

P   Let us confess our sinfulness to God and to each other and let us ask for God's mercy and forgiveness.

All   I confess...*(all pray the confiteor)*

Sing either "Kyrie Eleison" or "Domine Deus, Filius Patris, Miserere nobis" (Taizé Chants).

Act of Sorrow

O, my God, I am heartily sorry
for all my sins,
because I have offended thee,
who art infinitely good.
And I firmly resolve
with the help of thy grace,
Never to offend thee again.

P   May almighty God have mercy on us, forgive us our sinfulness, and bring us to the eternal kingdom of peace, love, and joy forever.

R   Amen.

P   Let us pray together to the Father, in the words Jesus taught us to use.

All Our Father ...

P   Let us now offer each other a sign of peace.

P   Let us thank God who shows us mercy and love through Jesus in the story of the prodigal son.

Be with us, Lord, as we go from here. Journey with us as we work to make your kingdom come in our own lives and in our world, through Christ Our Lord.

R   Amen.

Blessing

P   The Lord be with you.

R   And also with you.

P   May the God of Peace fill your hearts with every blessing. May God sustain you with gifts of hope and consolation. May God help you to offer your lives in God's service and bring you safely to eternal glory.

     May almighty God, the Father, the Son, ✠ and the Holy Spirit, grant you all that is good.

R   Amen.

YOUNG PEOPLE II

James Doherty

Theme: Eucharist

Begin with some quiet music or a hymn. A large crucifix is placed in the sanctuary. Two groups of two or three people each enter from opposite ends, dressed in dark clothes with dark jackets or pullovers. When they come face to face with each other, they take fixed positions and glare at each other. This position is held for a few minutes. Slowly they turn their heads until all their eyes are fixed on the crucifix. They hold this position. Then they slowly turn and look at each other again, and take off their jackets or tops to reveal white shirts or tops. They step towards each other, exchange greet-ings, and then simply kneel before the crucifix. As they kneel, the reading is proclaimed.

Gospel   Matthew 5:23–24

A reading from the holy Gospel according to Matthew.

If you are bringing your offering to the altar and there remember that your brother has something against you, leave your offering there before the altar, go and be reconciled with your brother first, and then come back and present your offering.

The gospel of the Lord.

R   Praise to you, Lord Jesus Christ.

Intercessions
For the times we have allowed our prejudices to dictate our actions.
Lord, have mercy. R

For the times we have closed our fists and our hearts to others.
Lord, have mercy. R

For the times we have refused to walk with our brothers and sisters. Lord, have mercy. R

Let us pray.
God our Father, enlighten our hearts and our minds with the light of your Holy Spirit. Keep us open to others journeying with us. Help us to be young enough to jump over the barriers of fear, prejudice, and hatred, so that our lives may continually witness to the life and love of Jesus Christ, your Son, who lives and reigns with you, in the unity of the Holy Spirit, one God for ever and ever.

R   Amen.

YOUNG PEOPLE III

James Doherty

Theme: Love your neighbor

Begin with a simple hymn. A Taizé chant is quite helpful.

Then a mime follows, involving four characters. One stands on a raised platform with arms outstretched to represent God the Father. Two stand a little distance away, deeply engrossed in conversation. A fourth enters carrying a weight on the shoulders (a simple log or piece of wood).

The person with the burden moves slowly towards the two who are conversing; they do not even notice. Then he or she moves toward the "God person," pauses, and looks up. The God person comes down to ground level, moves to the two persons talking, touches their shoulders, and points to the burdened person. They move slowly toward this person, remove the burden, and then all three walk side by side.

Reading   James 2:1–9

A reading from the letter of James.

My brothers, do not try to combine faith in Jesus Christ, our glorified Lord, with the making of distinctions between classes of people. Now suppose a man comes into your synagogue, beautifully dressed and with a gold ring on, and at the same time a poor man comes in, in shabby clothes, and you take notice of the well-dressed man, and say, "Come this way to the best seats"; then you tell the poor man, "Stand over there" or "You can sit on the floor by my footrest." Can't you see that you have used two different standards in your mind, and turned yourselves into judges, and corrupt judges at that?

Listen, my dear brothers: it was those who are poor according to the world that God chose, to be rich in faith and to be the heirs to the kingdom which he promised to those who love him. In spite of this, you have no respect for anybody who is poor. Isn't it always the rich who are against you? Isn't it always their doing when you are dragged before the court? Aren't they the ones who insult the honorable name to which you have been dedicated? Well, the right thing to do is to keep the supreme law of scripture: *you must love your neighbor as yourself*; but as soon as you make distinctions between classes of people, you are committing sin, and under condemnation for breaking the Law.

The word of the Lord.

R   Thanks be to God.

Intercessions

For the times we have closed our hearts to those in need.
Lord, have mercy. R

For the times that we have been so concerned about our own affairs that we have forgotten others.
Lord, have mercy. R

For the times that our own comfort has blinded us to the discomfort of others.
Lord, have mercy. R

Let us pray.
God our Father, teach us to be sensitive to the lives of others, help us to show them the respect that is their due, move us to respond to the needs of others, that we may learn to love you and our neighbor with one and the same love.
We make this prayer through Christ our Lord.

R   Amen.

CHILDREN I

Maura Hyland

INTRODUCTION

Opening Hymn
"Song of Hosea" (Glory and Praise *Vol. 3)*

P   The peace of Christ be with you all.

R   And also with you.

P   We have heard God's call to us to build a kingdom of peace,
love, truth, and justice. Through his Son, Jesus, God has shown
us how to do this. We know that there are many ways in which
we can build a better world at home, at school, and when we
are with our friends. Sometimes we work very hard to do this.
Sometimes, however, we are selfish and think only of ourselves
and of our own needs. When we stop and think about this, we
realize that we must change. Jesus tells us that God is always
waiting for us, always ready to forgive us. There is always time
to begin again.

LITURGY OF THE WORD

R   I Feel Ashamed (based on Psalm 130)

Today dear God, I come
Needing your forgiveness.
I do not feel good about myself
When I forget your laws.

But I remember your promise of mercy.
I wait for it just as I wait for a night storm to be over,
And daylight to come.
I know you will forgive me and not remember my sins.

P   Let us listen to a story from the gospel in which Jesus shows us the forgiveness and love of God.

Gospel   Luke 15:11–32

A reading from the holy Gospel according to Luke.

Jesus also said, "A man had two sons. The younger said to his father, 'Father, let me have the share of the estate that would come to me.' So the father divided the property between them. A few days later the younger son got together everything he had and left for a distant country where he squandered his money on a life of debauchery.

"When he had spent it all, that country experienced a severe famine, and now he began to feel the pinch, so he hired himself out to one of the local inhabitants who put him on his farm to feed the pigs. And he would willingly have filled his belly with the husks the pigs were eating but no one offered him anything. Then he came to his senses and said, 'How many of my father's paid servants have more food than they want, and here I am dying of hunger! I will leave this place and go to my father and say: Father, I have sinned against heaven and against you; I no longer deserve to be called your son; treat me as one of your paid servants.' So he left the place and went back to his father.

"While he was still a long way off, his father saw him and was moved with pity. He ran to the boy, clasped him in his arms and kissed him tenderly. Then his son said, 'Father, I have sinned against heaven and against you. I no longer deserve to be called your son.' But the father said to his servants, 'Quick! Bring out the best robe and put it on him; put a ring on his finger and sandals on his feet. Bring the calf we have been fattening, and kill it; we are going to have a feast, a celebration, because this son of mine was dead and has come back to life; he was lost and is found.' And they began to celebrate.

"Now the elder son was out in the fields, and on his way back, as he drew near the house, he could hear music and dancing. Calling one of the servants he asked what it was all about. 'Your brother has come,' replied the servant, 'and your father has killed the calf we had fattened because he has got him back safe and sound.' He was angry then and refused to go in, and his father came out to plead with him; but he answered his father, 'Look, all these years I have slaved for you and never once disobeyed your orders, yet you never offered me so much as a kid for me to celebrate with my friends. But, for this son of yours, when he comes back after swallowing up your property—he and his women—you kill the calf we had been fattening.'

"The father said, 'My son, you are with me always and all I have is yours. But it was only right we should celebrate and rejoice, because your brother here was dead and has come to life; he was lost and is found.'"

The gospel of the Lord.

R   Praise to you, Lord Jesus Christ.

Suggestions for Homily
The homilist might like to help the children to reflect on the following aspects of the story:

The prodigal son didn't appreciate all the good things he had in his father's house. It is very easy to take for granted the love and care and comfort that we find at home.

At first the prodigal son enjoyed himself with his new friends. Sometimes we enjoy what we're doing even if it is wrong.

He was very much ashamed when he became aware of what he had done, how ungrateful he was to his father, how selfishly he had acted. Sometimes we are ashamed of what we do, too. He must have found it very difficult to go back and say "I'm sorry." We, too, find it difficult to admit that we have been wrong.

The father did not condemn him or punish him as we would expect. He didn't make him a servant. He welcomed him back as a son. We find it difficult to understand the forgiveness of God. We find it difficult to believe that God really is ready to welcome us back no matter how bad we have been, no matter what wrongs we have done.

The older son was very jealous when he saw the fuss that was being made of his younger brother. Sometimes we too are jealous of others, of their success, or when people praise them.

Examination of Conscience

P   Let us take some time to think about our own lives and to ask ourselves if we have failed to answer God's call to build God's kingdom in our world.

Have we refused to build a better world at home:
Have we been selfish; have we refused to help out when we could; have we been conscious of the needs of others, especially those older or younger than ourselves; have we been the cause of fights and arguments; have we made up again after fights or have we held grudges; when we were wrong have we admitted that we were wrong and said we were sorry?
(Pause)

Have we refused to build a better world at school:
Have we cooperated with the teacher and with others in class when doing project work; have we refused to do our share of the tidying and cleaning in the classroom; have we done things that damage or destroy school property; have we been careless when using other people's books or pens or markers; have we taken other people's property and not returned it; have we refused to allow some children to join in games; have we ignored people who need our help; have we been disruptive in class?
(Pause)

Have we refused to build a better world in our neighborhood:
Have we been careless about throwing litter or damaging public property; have we refused to make an effort to help people who needed help, for example, by visiting old people; have we been careless on the road or done anything that would cause danger to ourselves or to others?
(Pause)

Have we refused to build a better world when we are playing with our friends:
Have we played fairly; have we caused fights and disagreements; have we done things to hurt others because of jealousy; have we told lies to our friends?
(Pause)

Have we remembered to say our prayers; have we been careless in church; have we tried to distract others during prayer time; have we used God's name or Jesus' name with disrespect? *(Pause)*

Act of Repentance

Hymn: *"Grant to Us, O Lord, a Heart Renewed."*

P   Let us confess to God that we have not always worked to build a better world, a world of love, truth, justice, and peace.

All   I confess ...*(all pray the confiteor)*

Child: For all the times when we have been selfish and, by thinking only of ourselves, have caused suffering to others. Lord, have mercy.

All   Lord, have mercy.

Child: For all the times when we have caused fights and arguments, when we have refused to say we are sorry, when we have not admitted that we were wrong when we told lies and were dishonest. Christ, have mercy.

All   Christ, have mercy.

Child: For all the times when we didn't bother to say our prayers, when we didn't pay attention at Mass, when we disturbed others, when we used God's name in disrespect. Lord, have mercy.

All   Lord, have mercy.

P   Let us pray together the Act of Sorrow.

All   O my God, I thank you for loving me...

P   Let us pray together in the words our Savior gave us:

All   Our Father ...

P   Let us offer each other a sign of peace.

P   Let us thank God our Father for forgiveness.

All   God our Father, thank you for forgiving me. Help me to love others. Help me to live as Jesus asked me to.

R   Amen.

Dismissal

P   Go in peace to listen to God's call to build a better world.

All   Amen.

P   Go in peace to bring God's love to others.

All   Amen.

P   May almighty God bless you, the Father, and the Son, ✠ and the Holy Spirit.

All   Amen.

Final Hymn

Sing "Make Me a Channel of Your Peace," or another appropriate song.

CHILDREN II

Pierce Murphy

Hymn
Sing "We Are Sorry, God," or another appropriate song.

Introduction
God our Father loves us. God loves us even when we are headstrong and do wrong. Like the loving Father in the gospel, God is always ready to forgive us. We come to God today to ask forgiveness. We promise God our love.

Prayer
Holy Spirit, help us to see ourselves as God sees us. Help us to find out what we have done wrong. Help us to be sorry, and give us the strength to live like Jesus.

Reader:
Jesus said: "Treat others as you would like them to treat you."

P   Jesus asks us to treat others well. When we hurt, insult, call names, ignore others, we are not treating them well.

     Have I treated my family and friends well?

Silence

P   Lord, have mercy.
All   Lord, have mercy.

Reader:
"Honor your father and your mother."

P   Jesus showed us how to honor and obey our parents. When we disobey our parents, do not help them, or are disrespectful we do not honor them.

     Have I honored my parents and those in charge of me?

Silence

P   Christ, have mercy.

All Christ, have mercy.

Reader:

Jesus said: "As long as you did this to one of these least ones, you did it to me."

P   Jesus invites us to be fair, to share and be generous with others, and to be friendly to all. When we steal, cause fights, or do not share we are not doing as Jesus asks.

Have I been mean, selfish, jealous, or dishonest?

Silence

P   Lord, have mercy.

All Lord, have mercy.

Reader:

Jesus said: "I am not alone, for the Father is always with me."

P   Jesus prayed to his Father every day. When we do not pray every day, rush our prayers, or use God's name outside of prayer, then we are not with God and Jesus.

Have I skipped my prayers, or used the name of God or Jesus when I should not?

Silence

P   Lord, have mercy.

All Lord, have mercy.

Act of Sorrow

All O my God, I thank you for loving me ...

P   Let us pray together as God's children:

All Our Father ...

P   We give a sign to each other that we love and forgive each other.

Individual Confession

If individual confession is omitted, the celebrant says the absolution prayer from the Mass.

Conclusion

Prayer after Confession (together)
God our Father, thank you for forgiving me.
Help me to love others.
Help me to live as Jesus asked me to.
Amen.

Prayer to the Holy Spirit (together)
Holy Spirit, I want to do what is right.
Help me.
Holy Spirit, I want to live like Jesus.
Guide me.
Holy Spirit, I want to pray like Jesus.
Teach me.

P   We ask Mary to help us live as good followers of Jesus as we say:

All   Hail Mary ...

P   May the blessing of God the Father, the Son, ✠ and the Holy Spirit be with you always.

Go in peace to live like Jesus.

R   Thanks be to God.

CHILDREN III

Sr. Francesca Kelly

Theme: Happiness

Opening Hymn

P   Peace and joy and happiness to all who gather here to ask forgiveness of their sins.

     Peace be with you.

All   And also with you.

P   Come, Holy Spirit, and renew in our hearts the desire to follow the Lord Jesus.

All   Come, Holy Spirit, come.

P   God wants us to be happy and God also wants our friends to be happy.

     Jesus was gentle with everyone and he wanted his friends to be gentle with each other. Then they would be happy and live in peace.

     "I leave you peace, I give you my own kind of peace," he said to his special friends. "Do not be worried or upset. Do not be afraid."

     Today, the Lord gives us his peace, and he wants us not to be worried or upset or afraid. He wants us to be happy and he tells us how we can be happy.

Reading and Reflection   Matthew 5:1–12

In the reading, Jesus tells us what we must do to be happy and to live in peace.

Child 1: How happy are the poor in spirit;
theirs is the kingdom of heaven. (Matthew 5:3)

P   (i) God wants you to know that you can be happy if you are trying to be good, kind, and loving.

(ii) God wants you to be happy with what you have, and not to be looking for more and more and more.

(iii) God wants you to share what you have with those who have not.

Child 2: Happy the gentle:
they shall have the earth for their heritage. (Matthew 5:4)

P   (i) God wants you to be patient, gentle, and kind when others annoy you.

(ii) God wants you to keep silent when you feel like saying something mean.

(iii) God wants you to keep silent when you feel like answering back.

Child 3: Happy those who mourn:
they shall be comforted. (Matthew 5:5)

P   (i) God wants your trust when you are sad and lonely.

(ii) God will be with you when your friends do not want you.

(iii) God will help you when you are sad and feeling down.

Child 4: Happy those who hunger and thirst for what is right:
they shall be satisfied. (Matthew 5:6)

P   (i) God wants you to treat others fairly.

(ii) God wants you to listen to your parents and to your teachers.

(iii) God wants you to pray — to speak to God each day.

Child 5: Happy the merciful:
they shall have mercy shown them. (Matthew 5:7)

P   (i) God wants you to forgive when you feel hurt, and when it is not easy.

(ii) God wants you to forgive when others do mean things to you on purpose.

(iii) God wants you to be kind and gentle to those who have hurt you.

Child 6: Happy the pure in heart:
they shall see God. (Matthew 5:8)

P   (i) God wants you to be good and honest, and not look for praise for the good you do.

(ii) God wants you to be kind, and not only to those who are kind to you.

(iii) God wants you to love, and not look for a reward.

Child 7: Happy the peacemakers:
they shall be called sons of God. (Matthew 5:9)

P   (i) God wants you to tell the truth.

(ii) God wants you to help others to be friends.

(iii) God wants you to make friends as soon as your quarrel is over.

Child 8: Happy those who are persecuted in the cause of right:
theirs is the kingdom of heaven. (Matthew 5:10)

P   (i) God wants you to do good even when others laugh at you.

(ii) God wants you to pray when others tell you "it's stupid."

(iii) God wants you to know that God will always be with you, when you are trying to do what God wants.

Examination of Conscience

P   We are happy when we do what God wants. Sometimes we do not do what God wants.

(i) Are you satisfied with what you have, or do you look for more and more and more?

(ii) Are you willing to share, or are you greedy and selfish?

(iii) Are you gentle and kind when others annoy you, or do you say mean things and answer back?

(iv) Are you ready to listen to your parents and teacher, or do you give trouble at home and at school?

(v) Are you ready to forgive when you are hurt, or do you hold grudges?

(vi) Are you ready to be good and honest, or do you look for praise and reward for any good you have done?

(vii) Are you ready to help others to be friends, and do you make up after a quarrel?

(viii) Are you ready to keep trying when others make fun of you, or do you feel ashamed and give up?

P   We have not done what God wants us to do. We have not loved. We are sorry. We confess that we have sinned.

All   I confess ...*(all pray the confiteor)*

P   God our Father, we did not do what you wanted us to do. We ask you to listen to our prayer of sorrow.

All   O my God ...

P   God our Father, we your children ask you to keep us in your love and care. Forgive us, as we say *(or sing)* the prayer that Jesus taught us:

All   Our Father ...

Blessing

P   May God the Father be good to us, forgive us all that we have done wrong, and one day make us happy with God in our home in heaven.

All Amen.

P   Go in peace to love God,
     to be happy yourselves,
     and to help others to be happy also.

All Amen.

Hymn

CHRISTIAN UNITY

THE SPINNING TOP
Robin Boyd

Lord, we are so top-heavy—our whole structure
In session, Synod, Council and Assembly—
The whole thing topples, and to keep from falling
We, top-like, spin and spin on our own axis,
Self-centered, humming, whipped to static fury,
And so gyrating pride ourselves on action.

Lord, knock us sideways, send us spinning outwards;
Uncenter us from self, and make our axis
That transverse axle-tree, the Cross, that turning
On Christ alone we may roll forward, steady,
To that great day when, every creature gospeled,
The End shall come, and nations see the glory.

Kohlapur, India 1962.

CHRISTIAN UNITY I

Alan Falconer

This service is excerpted and used with the permission of RTÉ radio, which broadcast it in December 1980. The service is conducted by a Protestant (CI) and a Catholic (CII) celebrant.

Invocation
Hymn or psalm with the Theme: God's gifts to us.

CII: In the light of God's gifts to us, each of us is aware that we have failed to live as God intended, both in our individual lives and as communities. Therefore, let us offer our prayers of thanksgiving and confession to God:

CI: All glory, praise, and honor to you, O God our Father,
for creating us,
for giving us the gifts of life and love,
for daily nourishing us.

CII: All glory, praise, and honor to you,
Jesus Christ our Divine Redeemer,
for drawing us into oneness with yourself
in the unity of the Father and the Spirit,
through your cross and resurrection freeing us from bondage,
enabling us to live in liberty subject to no one,
enabling us to live in freedom subject and servant to all people.

CI: All glory, praise, and honor to you, Spirit Divine,
for enabling us to cry "Abba"—Father,
for illuminating our minds and understanding,
for giving us the strength to love.

CII: We adore you, God, Father, Son, and Holy Spirit.

CI: We acknowledge you to be Lord.

(Pause)

CII: Lord, have mercy on us.
As Roman Catholics,
we have been slow to acknowledge the faith and love of members of other Christian traditions; preferring to remain behind the wall of separation; preferring to proclaim that outside our boundaries there is no salvation; too often we have lived without any reference to the members of other Christian traditions, preferring to press for the implementation of our needs—in matters of the family, education, and the welfare of society, we have been quick to point out the failures of others, and slow to acknowledge our own inadequacies.
Lord have mercy on us.

(Pause)

May God forgive us our sins of omission and commission,
may God strengthen us by the Spirit,
may God keep us in eternal life
through Jesus Christ the Son, our Lord.

R Amen.

A prayer in similar tone from the Protestant celebrant follows here.

Hymn: *Theme: Glory to God.*

Readings   Ephesians 2:11–22

A reading from the letter to the Ephesians.

Do not forget, then, that there was a time when you who were pagans physically, termed the Uncircumcised by those who speak of themselves as the Circumcision by reason of a physical operation, do not forget, I say, that you had no Christ and were excluded from membership of Israel, aliens with no part in the covenants with their

Promise; you were immersed in this world, without hope and without God. But now in Christ Jesus, you that used to be so far apart from us have been brought very close, by the blood of Christ. For he is the peace between us, and has made the two into one and broken down the barrier which used to keep them apart, actually destroying in his own person the hostility caused by the rules and decrees of the Law. This was to create one single New Man in himself out of the two of them and by restoring peace through the cross, to unite them both in a single Body and reconcile them with God. In his own person he killed the hostility. Later he came to bring the good news of peace, *peace to you who were far away and peace to those who were near at hand.* Through him, both of us have in the one Spirit our way to come to the Father.

So you are no longer aliens or foreign visitors: you are citizens like all the saints, and part of God's household. You are part of a building that has the apostles and prophets for its foundations, and Christ Jesus himself for its main cornerstone. As every structure is aligned on him, all grow into one holy temple in the Lord; and you too, in him, are being built into a house where God lives, in the Spirit.

The word of the Lord.

R   Thanks be to God.

Gospel   John 1:1–5, 6–14

A reading from the holy Gospel according to John.

In the beginning was the Word:
the Word was with God
and the Word was God.
He was with God in the beginning.
Through him all things came to be,
not one thing had its being but through him.
All that came to be had life in him
and that life was the light of men,
a light that shines in the dark,
a light that darkness could not overpower.

A man came, sent by God.
His name was John.
He came as a witness,
as a witness to speak for the light,
so that everyone might believe through him.
He was not the light,
only a witness to speak for the light.

The Word was the true light
that enlightens all men;
and he was coming into the world.
He was in the world
that had its being through him,
and the world did not know him.
He came to his own domain
and his own people did not accept him.
But to all who did accept him
he gave power to become children of God,
to all who believe in the name of him
who was born not out of human stock
or urge of the flesh
or will of man
but of God himself.
The Word was made flesh,
he lived among us,
and we saw his glory,
the glory that is his as the only Son of the Father,
full of grace and truth.

The gospel of the Lord.

R   Praise to you, Lord Jesus Christ.

Meditation

The text for our meditation this morning is from the passage read earlier from the letter to the Ephesians:

For he is the peace between us, and has made the two into one and broken down the barrier which used to keep them apart, actually destroying in his own person the hostility caused by the rules and decrees of the Law. This was to create one single New Man in himself out of the two of them and by restoring peace through the cross, to unite them both in a single Body and reconcile them with God.

Collect
May the words of my mouth
and the whisperings of our hearts
always find favor in your presence.
Lord God, our Rock—our Redeemer.
Amen.

All too often, we, as Christians, have been happy to live with a caricature of other traditions. Each of us has been content with a caricature of Christianity. We, who should have known better, have not risen to the challenge and opportunities presented. Within our different traditions, we have been so sure that we possess the truth. We have been so convinced that we are the saved and are in a right relationship to God that we have not sought or expected to hear the challenge of the gospel from beyond the walls and boundaries erected by our preconceived ideas. We have even gone so far as to label members of other Christian churches as either non-Christians, at worst, or less than Christian at best. All of us have made of Christianity a rather private or personal affair: Christianity is about my salvation; it is about my relationship to God.

We have failed to respond in faith and love to the One who was crucified precisely because he challenged the values, traditions, and caricatures of various groups in the society of his day. He challenged the society of his day by his openness, his concern for others, particularly those who had been dismissed by the society of his day, those who had been killed because of a caricature—the lepers, the widows, the poor, the prisoners.

All of this demands our repentance; that is, it requires of us not just a readiness to confess our sins. It requires of us also a commitment to a new life. Is not the message of Christmas precisely that new life is found in the most unexpected places? Does not the gospel point us to the fact time and time again that it is in the midst of suffering, of hopelessness, of crisis that the birth of hope takes place?—that the vision of New Life emerges?

The Israel of Jesus' day was plagued by group rivalries, by economic imbalance, by distorted values. Israel as a nation was under the occupation of the Romans, in whose hands political power and control resided. There was no real contact between Romans and Jews except out of administrative or economic necessity. Each group resented the other: to the Romans, Jews were an uncivilized and uncultured people; to the Jews, the Romans were a military power who had no idea of what it was to serve God and to have an awareness of a Being more powerful than any human power, more just than any human system of justice.

Among the Jews themselves there were a number of factions, each of which regarded itself as unique or exclusive for one reason or another. The Samaritans and the Jews had had intense rivalry for years—the Samaritans claimed a more direct line of succession to the first High Priest. So intense had this rivalry and hatred become that a group of Samaritans had strewn the bones of dead dogs in the inner sanctuary of the Temple on the night before one of the great Passover feasts, thus making it impossible for the Jews to celebrate their feast since the Temple itself was ritually unclean. This had happened in the generation before Jesus and was in retaliation for the burning of the Samaritan temple by the Jews. Feelings still ran high between Samaritan and Jew.

Within the Jews there were also factions: the Essene community, a small monastic community, asserted that only by following their religious rule could salvation be acquired. The rivalry between the priests and the other religious was firmly established through questions of who had the best ancestry of priesthood, who were therefore closest to God, who were the best interpreters of the Law? The religious rivalries were also matched by economic groups. A large merchant class arose in Jerusalem, which depended for its livelihood on the Court and on the Temple. Anyone who said anything against these institutions was attacking their livelihood. And a similar group of merchants arose in Caesarea to serve the Roman occupation. They looked with disdain on the poor backward folk in the provinces. Each group was only capable of asserting its own viewpoint. Each group was self-contained—it could learn nothing from anyone else. Indeed, anyone who did listen to another group was suspect. It is not that people then were particularly evil. It is just that they had false priorities, as we can see in the light of Jesus. They were self-assured. They had defined themselves against others.

It was into this situation that Jesus was born. His whole life was a challenge to these priorities. His birth took place in economic squalor and his ministry was directed to the poor, the have-nots. His life and ministry invited people to transcend their preconceptions and their cherished convictions. He admired the faith of a Roman soldier; he spoke with a Samaritan; indeed, in his most famous parable, a Samaritan figures as an example of how God would have us live; he brought wholeness to lepers and to other physically and mentally handicapped people—normally outcasts of society; he gathered around him a group composed mainly of unsophisticated provincials; he questioned the priorities of the religious experts—theologians and churchmen—of his day. Ultimately, he was crucified because he had transcended and challenged these self-assured divisions. In his own person he had shown forth God's peace, God's shalom, whereby God, in God's relationship with God's people, had brought wholeness. He had shown his people that his way was the way of inclusiveness and openness. This peace, so apparent in Jesus, was concerned with the whole of society, with every facet of its life—economic, political, social—and society was to be a reflection of God's care for us. It is for this reason that the Ephesians passage speaks of Jesus being the Peace between us, bringing hitherto alienated groups into unity in Jesus. This was a reality for the early church and is to be a reality for us. This peace is a reality for us in the baby Jesus. This peace is also our task today, not just so that Christians might enjoy the chumminess of such a life of wholeness, of living together, but so that they might be peacemakers. The German pastor

Dietrich Bonhoeffer, when he commented on the Beatitude, "Happy the peacemakers," had this to say:

> The followers of Jesus have been called to peace, for when he called them they found their peace, for he is their peace. But now they are told that they must not only have peace but make it ... Now they are partners in Christ's work of reconciliation. They are called the sons of God as he is the Son of God.

It is only by taking the birth of Jesus really seriously that we have any possibility of overcoming the deep divisions in our society. The challenge of the birth of Jesus, to the Christian and the churches, is to re-examine our priorities asking whether we are really prepared to love others in the costly way of Jesus—whether we are prepared to transcend our religious, political, economic, and social groups, and work for the well-being of our whole society. May God give us all the strength for this task. Amen.

CII: Let us reaffirm together our commitment to God by saying together the Apostles' Creed.

Hymn: *Theme: Unity of the church for the unity of humankind.*

Intercessions

CII:　God, Father, Son, and Holy Spirit, in this world of ours of alienation and fragmentation, we pray for those who work for peace, who bring wholeness and healing, asking that you will strengthen us as we try to support them.

CI:　For all working in medicine, whether dealing with the temporarily ill, the physically or mentally disabled, or the terminally ill.

CII:　For all working among the marginalized in society—the travellers, the children living in poverty, the refugees, the homeless.

CI:　For all working in education, that the search for understanding and love may dominate them and through them inspire others.

CII:　For all working in the media, that balanced reporting of events may help our society to face up to its own responsibilities for caring and sharing.

CI: For the agencies and agents of reconciliation, that their work might heal divisions between and within societies.

CII: O God, at this time, as we give you thanks for the birth of Jesus, the Prince of Peace, your Son, our Lord, who was born in poverty, who brought hope to people experiencing hopelessness, who dispelled fear through love and compassion, who gave wholeness and healing to all people, grant that we may be worthy to continue his work to the glory of your name.

CI: Grant to each of us as individuals, and to us as a community, a pure heart that we may see you, a humble heart that we may hear you, a heart of love that we may serve you, a heart of faith that we may always live in you, and, with the saints of all ages and all places, enable us to say:

All Our Father...

CII: As a symbol of reconciliation, let us offer each other a sign of peace.

Hymn: *Theme: Our service in the world.*

Final Blessing

CHRISTIAN UNITY II

Sean Collins, OFM

Theme: The scandal of the disunity of Christians

It is envisaged that the gathering will take place in silence, or perhaps with muted instrumental music. Ministers do not enter in procession, but take their places singly and unobtrusively. The participants stand, kneel, and sit as considered appropriate. When all is ready, a minister says:

P   Blessed is the Kingdom of the Father, and of the Son, and of the Holy Spirit, now and ever, and unto ages of ages.

R   Amen.

Two readers read the following, and the congregation answers each time:

Reader 1: My people, what have I done to you? How have I offended you?
Answer me.

All   Holy God, Holy and Strong, Holy Immortal One, have mercy on us.

Reader 2: I came in love to Bethlehem to take you on my shoulders and carry you to Paradise: and you have preferred rejection and strife to peace and goodwill.

All   Holy God, Holy and Strong, Holy Immortal One, have mercy on us.

Reader 1: I went down into Jordan river with your sins upon me, that you might rise from the water of baptism in innocence restored: and you fail to recognize my gift when given to another.

All   Holy God, Holy and Strong, Holy Immortal One, have mercy on us.

Reader 2: I went about doing good, with healing in my hands and comfort in my eyes: yet you avert your eyes from your own sisters and brothers.

All Holy God, Holy and Strong, Holy Immortal One, have mercy on us.

Reader 1: I gathered you, my little flock, as the mother hen enfolds her chicks, and the shepherd his sheep and lambs: but you have spurned that enfolding, and gone astray.

All Holy God, Holy and Strong, Holy Immortal One, have mercy on us.

Reader 2: I gave myself equally to all, in bread and cup poured out and shared: and even this, my precious gift, you made a sign of contradiction.

All Holy God, Holy and Strong, Holy Immortal One, have mercy on us.

Reader 1: On Golgotha I died in ransom for your sins, that I might gather the scattered children of the Father: and you remain divided, O my people.

All Holy God, Holy And Strong, Holy Immortal One, have mercy on us.

Reader 2: On the third day I arose in glory and breathed on you the Spirit of unity and pardon: yet you continue to grieve God's Holy Spirit.

All Holy God, Holy and Strong, Holy Immortal One, have mercy on us.

Reader 1: Behold, I am with you all days, that you may be one as I and the Father are one, so that the world may believe: my people, hear my voice and follow me, that there may be one flock and one shepherd.

All O Shepherd of Israel, hear us;
let your face shine on us
and we shall be saved.
Holy God, Holy and Strong, Holy Immortal One,
have mercy on us.

A minister says:

Let us pray.

Almighty, ever-living God, it is your will that in your beloved Son, Jesus Christ, all creation be made new and restored to joy.

Grant to us, your wayward children, such a lively awareness of our failure to be Christ's co-workers in so great a task that we may be seized by sorrow for what is past, and urgency for the work that lies ahead.

Rekindle in us, Gracious Lord, that longing for unity and for the spread of the gospel that alone can erase the hurt of the past and harness all our efforts, together, toward the coming of your kingdom; through Jesus Christ our Lord.

R   Amen.

All are invited to listen to God's word.

First Reading   Hosea 12:1–9

The tender love of our God will bend down to us once more, for we are his.

A reading from the book of Hosea.

All around me are the lies of Ephraim
and the deceit of the House of Israel.
Ephraim feeds on the wind,
forever chasing the wind from the East,
accumulating falsehood and fraud,
making treaties with Assyria,
sending oil to Egypt.

Yahweh has a case against Israel,
he will pay Jacob as his conduct merits,
and will repay him as his deeds deserve.
In the very womb he supplanted his brother,
in maturity he wrestled against God.
He wrestled with the angel and beat him,
he wept and pleaded with him.

He met him at Bethel
and there God spoke to him.
Yes, Yahweh God of Sabaoth, Yahweh is his name.
Turn again, then, to your God,
hold fast to love and justice,
and always put your trust in your God.

Canaan holds fraudulent scales in his hands,
to defraud is his delight.
"How rich I have become!" says Ephraim,
"I have amassed a fortune."
But he will keep nothing of all his profits,
because of the guilt that he has brought on himself.

I have been Yahweh, your God, since the days in the land of Egypt.
I will make you live in tents again
as on the day of Meeting.

The word of the Lord.

R   Thanks be to God.

Song
"The Song of Hosea," or any song of repentance and return.

Second Reading   1 Corinthians 1:10–17
The only source of salvation is the cross of Christ, beneath which we all stand.

A reading from the first letter to the Corinthians.

I do appeal to you, brothers, for the sake of our Lord Jesus Christ, to make up the differences between you, and instead of disagreeing among yourselves, to be united again in your belief and practice. From what Chloe's people have been telling me, my dear brothers, it is clear that there are serious differences among you. What I mean are all these slogans that you have like: "I am for Paul," "I am for Apollos," "I am for Cephas," "I am for Christ." Has Christ been parceled out? Was it Paul that was crucified for you? Were you baptized in the name of Paul? I am thankful that I never baptized any of you after Crispus and Gaius so none of you can say he was baptized in my name. Then there was the family of Stephanas, of course, that I bapized too, but no one else as far as I can remember.

For Christ did not send me to baptize, but to preach the Good News, and not to preach that in the terms of philosophy in which the crucifixion of Christ cannot be expressed.

The word of the Lord.

R   Thanks be to God.

Song
Any song that stresses the love of God in Christ Jesus is appropriate.

Third Reading   John 15:1–17
A reading from the holy Gospel according to John.

I am the true vine,
and my Father is the vinedresser,
Every branch in me that bears no fruit
he cuts away,
and every branch that does bear fruit he prunes
to make it bear even more.
You are pruned already,
by means of the word that I have spoken to you.
Make your home in me, as I make mine in you.
As a branch cannot bear fruit all by itself,
but must remain part of the vine,
neither can you unless you remain in me.
I am the vine,
you are the branches.
Whoever remains in me, with me in him,
bears fruit in plenty;
for cut off from me you can do nothing.
Anyone who does not remain in me
is like a branch that has been thrown away
—he withers;

these branches are collected and thrown on the fire,
and they are burned.
If you remain in me
and my words remain in you,
you may ask what you will
and you shall get it.
It is to the glory of my Father that you should bear much fruit,
and then you will be my disciples.
As the Father has loved me,
so I have loved you.
Remain in my love.
If you keep my commandments
you will remain in my love,
just as I have kept my Father's commandments
and remain in his love.
I have told you this
so that my own joy may be in you
and your joy be complete.
This is my commandment:
love one another,
as I have loved you.
A man can have no greater love
than to lay down his life for his friends.
You are my friends,
if you do what I command you.
I shall not call you servants any more,
because a servant does not know
his master's business;
I call you friends,
because I have made known to you
everything I have learned from my Father.
You did not choose me,
no, I chose you;
and I commissioned you
to go out and to bear fruit,
fruit that will last;

and then the Father will give you
anything you ask him in my name.
What I command you
is to love one another.

The gospel of the Lord.

R   Praise to you, Lord Jesus Christ.

One of the ministers gives the homily, or, depending on the size of the group, a shared reflection on the word of God may take place.

Litany of Repentance
A minister or cantor reads or sings the litany, and all respond.

P   In peace, let us pray to the Lord.
R   Kyrie eleison *or* Lord, have mercy.

For the peace from above, and for our salvation, let us pray to the Lord. R

For the peace of the whole world and of all men and women everywhere, let us pray to the Lord. R

For the unity of Christians for whom Christ died, let us pray to the Lord. R

For the leaders of all the churches, that they may have the courage to face the risk of misunderstanding in the quest for Christian unity, let us pray to the Lord. R

That we may put aside the bitter memory of past insult and scorn, and make room in our hearts for Christ's forgiving love, let us pray to the Lord. R

That the steadfastness of our ancestors in their religious convictions may inspire us to seek the truth God offers us now, even when accepting it costs us pain, let us pray to the Lord. R

That the Lord may preserve us from thinking that we alone have all the truth, let us pray to the Lord. R

That conflict and hatred that appeal to religion and breed on past wounds be banished like a plague from among us, let us pray to the Lord. R

That our children may inherit a faith that is strong and Christ-centered, and open in love to all his followers, let us pray to the Lord. R

That the prayer of Jesus, "May all be one," may never be erased from our minds, and that we may never be guilty of delaying its fulfillment by thought, or word, or deed, let us pray to the Lord. R

That we may put aside our indifference and our pride, and begin to do all in our power to heal the scandal of our divisions, that the world may believe, let us pray to the Lord. R

Another Minister:

Therefore, let us commend ourselves, and one another, and our whole life to Christ our God:

R   To you, O Lord.

For to you belong all glory, honor, and worship, to the Father, and to the Son, and to the Holy Spirit, now and ever, and unto ages of ages.

R   Amen.

All keep silence for a time. Then a minister leads a common confession:

Minister: God, our Father,

All   we confess that we have sinned against you, and that we have failed to preserve the unity of the Spirit in the bond of peace. We have not loved you with our whole heart. We have allowed the power you have planted in us to remain fruitless. We have exhausted our energies in shallow rivalry, and allowed our prejudice to blind us to your presence in our brothers and sisters. Forgive all that is past; send forth anew your Holy Spirit upon us; and bind us into a living fellowship to the glory of your Holy Name, through Jesus Christ our Lord. Amen.

Minister: As we repent of our failures in the past, we take hope from the unity we have already achieved. Let us listen to the picture of the church as she can be, proposed by representatives of all our Communities in the Lima Statement:

Reader: In a broken world, God calls the whole of humanity to become God's people. For this purpose, God chose Israel and then spoke in a unique and decisive way in Jesus Christ, God's Son ... The life of the church is based on Christ's victory over the powers of evil and death, accomplished once for all. Christ offers forgiveness, invites to repentance and delivers from destruction. Through Christ, people are enabled to turn in praise to God and in service to their neighbors. In Christ, they find the source of new life in freedom, mutual forgiveness, and love. Through Christ, their hearts and minds are directed to the consummation of the kingdom where Christ's victory will become manifest and all things made new. God's purpose is that, in Christ, all people should share in this fellowship. The church lives through the liberating and renewing power of the Holy Spirit ... The Spirit calls people to faith, sanctifies them through many gifts, gives them strength to witness to the Gospel, and empowers them to serve in hope and love. The Spirit keeps the church in the truth and guides it despite the frailty of its members. The church is called to proclaim and prefigure the kingdom of God. It accomplishes this by announcing the Gospel to the world and by its very existence as the body of Christ ... The members of Christ's body are to struggle with the oppressed towards that freedom and dignity promised with the coming of the kingdom. This mission needs to be carried out in varying political, social, and cultural contexts. In order to fulfil this mission faithfully, they will seek relevant forms of witness and service in each situation. In so doing they bring to the world a foretaste of the joy and glory of God's kingdom.

Minister: As we look to the coming of the kingdom, let us pray with one heart and one voice the words our blessed Savior gave us:

All Our Father ...

Minister: As a pledge of our earnest intent to pursue all that makes for peace and for mutual upbuilding, let us exchange a sign of peace.

The peace is exchanged in whatever manner seems appropriate.

Minister: And so to God who has the power to do so much more than we can ask or even conceive, to God be glory in the church and in Christ Jesus, from generation to generation evermore.

R   Amen.

Minister: Go forth in peace.

R   In the name of Christ. Amen.

A song of the mystery of the church is sung, for example, "Thy Hand, O Lord, Has Guided" (to Thornbury) or "The Church's One Foundation" (to Aurelia).

ON A PILGRIMAGE
to a local place of pilgrimage

To be adapted to local traditions and conditions

Oliver Crilly

P   In the name of the Father, and of the Son, and of the Holy Spirit.

R   Amen.

Introduction

Opening Prayer

P   Lord, as we gather at _____ today,
we thank you
for the faith of our people who have gone before us.
We thank you for the gifts you have given to each person here,
and especially for the people you have placed around us in our
lives.
We pray, through the intercession of St. _____,
for forgiveness for our sins
and for healing of all our hurts
and illnesses of mind and body.
We make our prayer with confidence
through Jesus Christ our Lord.

R   Amen.

LITURGY OF THE WORD

First Reading   Romans 12:1–2, 9–19
Be transformed by the renewal of your mind.

A reading from the letter of Paul to the Romans.

Think of God's mercy, my brothers, and worship him, I beg you, in a way that is worthy of thinking beings, by offering your living bodies as a holy sacrifice, truly pleasing to God. Do not model yourselves on the behavior of the world around you, but let your behavior change, modeled by your new mind. This is the only way to discover the will of God and know what is good, what it is that God wants, what is the perfect thing to do.

Do not let your love be a pretense, but sincerely prefer good to evil. Love each other as much as brothers should, and have a profound respect for each other. Work for the Lord with untiring effort and with great earnestness of spirit. If you have hope, this will make you cheerful. Do not give up if trials come; and keep on praying. If any of the saints are in need you must share with them; and you should make hospitality your special care.

Bless those who persecute you: never curse them, bless them. Rejoice with those who rejoice and be sad with those in sorrow. Treat everyone with equal kindness; never be condescending but make real friends with the poor.

The word of the Lord.

R   Thanks be to God.

Responsorial Psalm   Psalm 98:1–9
R   The Lord has remembered his mercy.

Sing Yahweh a new song
for he has performed marvels,
his own right hand, his holy arm,
gives him the power to save. R

Yahweh has displayed his power;
has revealed his righteousness to the nations.
mindful of his love and faithfulness
to the house of Israel. R

The most distant parts of the earth have seen
the saving power of our God.
Acclaim Yahweh, all the earth,
burst into shouts of joy. R

Alleluia
Alleluia, alleluia,
Speak Lord, your servants are listening;
you have the words of eternal life.
Alleluia.

Gospel   Mark 12:28–34
A reading from the holy Gospel according to Mark.

One of the scribes who had listened to them debating and had observed how well Jesus had answered them, now came up and put a question to him, "Which is the first of all the commandments?" Jesus replied, "This is the first: *Listen, Israel, the Lord our God is the one Lord, and you must love the Lord your God with all your heart, with all your soul*, with all your mind and *with all your strength*. The second is this: *You must love your neighbor as yourself*. There is no commandment greater than these." The scribe said to him, "Well spoken, Master; what you have said is true: that he is one and there is no other. To love him with all your heart, with all your understanding and strength, and to love your neighbor as yourself, this is far more important than any holocaust or sacrifice." Jesus, seeing how wisely he had spoken, said, "You are not far from the kingdom of God." And after that no one dared to question him any more.

The gospel of the Lord.

R   Praise to you, Lord Jesus Christ.

Suggestions for Homily
— life of the saint
— local associations and history
— symbolism (e.g. water from a holy well, St Brigid's Cross, High Cross, monastic life, etc.)
— saints are sinners who loved: We also are God's pilgrim people, weak, sinful, but trusting in God's love.

Prayer of the Faithful

P   Let us pray to the Lord,
    who is enthroned on the praises of his people.
    Let us thank him for this place,
    for the life of St. _____
    and for this day.

    Let us thank him for all our people and for everyone gathered
    here, remembering that thankfulness works miracles.

    For everyone here present, for our families and friends, for
    those we particularly want to pray for, that God will bless us
    all, through the intercession of St. _____. Lord, hear us.

R   Lord, graciously hear us.

    We pray for the healing of physical illness, that God's healing
    power may touch all who are suffering in body, and heal them.
    Lord, hear us. R

    For those suffering in mind or personality, we pray that God
    will drive away all anguish, pain, hurt, and depression, and
    give them peace of mind and peace of soul. Lord, hear us. R

    For the healing of relationships, we pray that God will ease ten-
    sions in families or between neighbors, and that where there is
    hatred, God may bring love. Lord, hear us. R

    Let us pause in silence so that all may pray in the depths of
    their hearts.

P   Father, we offer all our prayers through the intercession of St.
    _____ and Our Lady and all the saints, and we offer them
    with confidence through Jesus Christ our Lord.

R   Amen.

Litany

Father in Heaven	have mercy on us
Jesus Christ, redeemer of the world	have mercy on us
Holy Spirit, our guide and consoler	have mercy on us

Holy Trinity, one God	have mercy on us
Mary conceived without sin	intercede for us
Mary, assumed into Heaven	intercede for us
Together with all sinners	we cry unto you, O Lord
Together with the sick and injured	"
Together with the lonely	"
Together with the heartbroken	"
Together with the bereaved	"
Together with the poor	"
Together with the oppressed	"
Together with the rejected	"
Together with the homeless	"
Together with the disabled	"
Together with the unemployed	"
Together with all who are broken or maimed in spirit	"
In the name of all who are sad	"
In the name of all who are afraid	"
In the name of all who are angry	"
In the name of all who are joyful	"
That we may love and be loved as you prayed	"
That we may belong to one another as true disciples	"
That we may live responsibly in our relationships	"
That we may recognize the worth of everyone we meet	"
Together with St. _____	"
(add other saints as appropriate)	
Together with all the holy men and women	"

Let us pray.
Lord, grant us the grace we need through the intercession of the saints. May we merit to be their fellow citizens in heaven.
We ask this through Christ our Lord.

R   Amen.

THE SACRAMENT OF PENANCE

Preparation for Confession

P   My brothers and sisters, let us confess our sins and pray for each other, that we may be healed.

All   I confess...*(all pray the confiteor)*

P   Let us now pray to our Father in the words our Savior gave us:

All   Our Father...

P   God our Father, we, your children, confess our sins and beg your forgiveness. Through the ministry of your church, forgive us our sins, renew our Spirit that we may give you thanks and praise.
We ask this through Jesus the Lord.

R   Amen.

Individual Confession

The Rosary may be recited by the group during individual confessions.

Prayer of Thanksgiving

Father, we thank you for the faith of our people. We thank you for the traditions of penance and pilgrimage that they have handed on to us. We go through life as your pilgrim people. Help us to accept the limitations we find in ourselves and those around us. May we always trust in your love and mercy.
We ask this through Jesus Christ our Lord.

R   Amen.

Final Blessing

P   The peace of the Father, Son, and Holy Spirit, be with you night and day.

R   Amen.

P   May you be in the care of the Father, Son, and Holy Spirit, every day and night of your lives.

R   Amen.

P   The blessing of the Father, Son, and Holy Spirit be with you now and forever.

R   Amen.

P   And may almighty God bless you, the Father, Son, ✠ and Holy Spirit.

R   Amen.

P   Let us go in the peace of Christ.

R   Amen.

AT A WAKE

Andrew McCloskey

Where it is customary to have the Rosary late in the evening at a wake, this service could introduce confessions after the Rosary has been recited. Or it might be used at any time of the day according to local circumstances.

Sign of the Cross

P   The Lord be with you.

R   And also with you.

Introduction

We are going to have confessions now for anyone who wants to take the opportunity of receiving the sacrament, but first we will take a few minutes to prepare together. Let us listen to a short Scripture reading:

They are at peace.

A reading from the book of Wisdom.   Wisdom 3:1–9

The souls of the virtuous are in the hands of God,
no torment shall ever touch them.
In the eyes of the unwise, they did appear to die,
their going looked like a disaster,
their leaving us, like annihilation;
but they are in peace.

or

All who believe in Jesus will have their sins forgiven through his name.

A reading from the Acts of the Apostles.   Acts 10:36, 42–43

It is true, God sent his word to the people of Israel, and it was to them that *the good news of peace was brought* by Jesus Christ—but Jesus

Christ is Lord of all. He has ordered us to proclaim this to his people and to tell them that God has appointed him to judge everyone, alive or dead. It is to him that all the prophets bear this witness: that all who believe in Jesus will have their sins forgiven through his name.

or

I am the resurrection and the life.

A reading from the holy Gospel according to John.   John 11:21–27

Jesus said:

"I am the resurrection.
If anyone believes in me, even though he dies he will live,
and whoever lives and believes in me
will never die."

and/or

Responsorial Psalm   Psalm 130

R   From the depths I call to you, Yahweh.

1.   From the depths I call to you, Yahweh,
        Lord, listen to my cry for help!
        Listen compassionately
        to my pleading. R

2.   If you never overlooked our sins, Yahweh,
        Lord, could anyone survive?
        But you do forgive us:
        and for that we revere you. R

3.   I wait for Yahweh, my soul waits for him,
        I rely on his promise,
        My soul is longing for the Lord
        more than a watchman on the coming of dawn. R

4.   For it is with Yahweh that mercy is to be found;
        and a generous redemption;
        it is he who redeems Israel
        from all their sins. R

A few words of reflection may be added:
— Death of a person causes us to reflect on our dependence on God and on God's mercy.
— Where our dead brother/sister has gone, we too will have to go; our journey of life ends in death. Part of our journey is to seek reconciliation with God and with each other.
— Going to confession helps us to be prepared to participate fully in the funeral liturgy, to receive communion, to unite our prayers with the family and friends who mourn...There is no more helpful thing we can do for them at this time.

Pause for brief examination of conscience.

All say:
I confess...*(all pray the confiteor)*

All say together:
Our Father ...

The priest concludes:
Let us pray.
Father, we thank you for your love and mercy.
Help us now to make a good confession,
and forgive us all our sins.
Help us to live good lives
that we may one day all be united
in the kingdom of your love.

R   Amen.

Individual confessions now follow.